COMPLEMENTS

for Benjamin and Jocelyn

COMPLEMENTS

eloquence of small objects

photographs and text

Patricia Z. Smith

foreword

David Hume Kennerly

design

Louise Brody

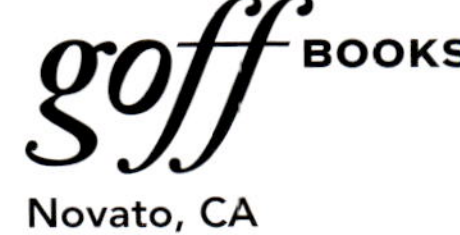

Novato, CA

The creation of something new is not accomplished by the intellect but by the play instinct acting from inner necessity. The creative mind plays with the objects it loves. Without this playing with fantasy no creative work has ever yet come to birth.

—C. G. Jung

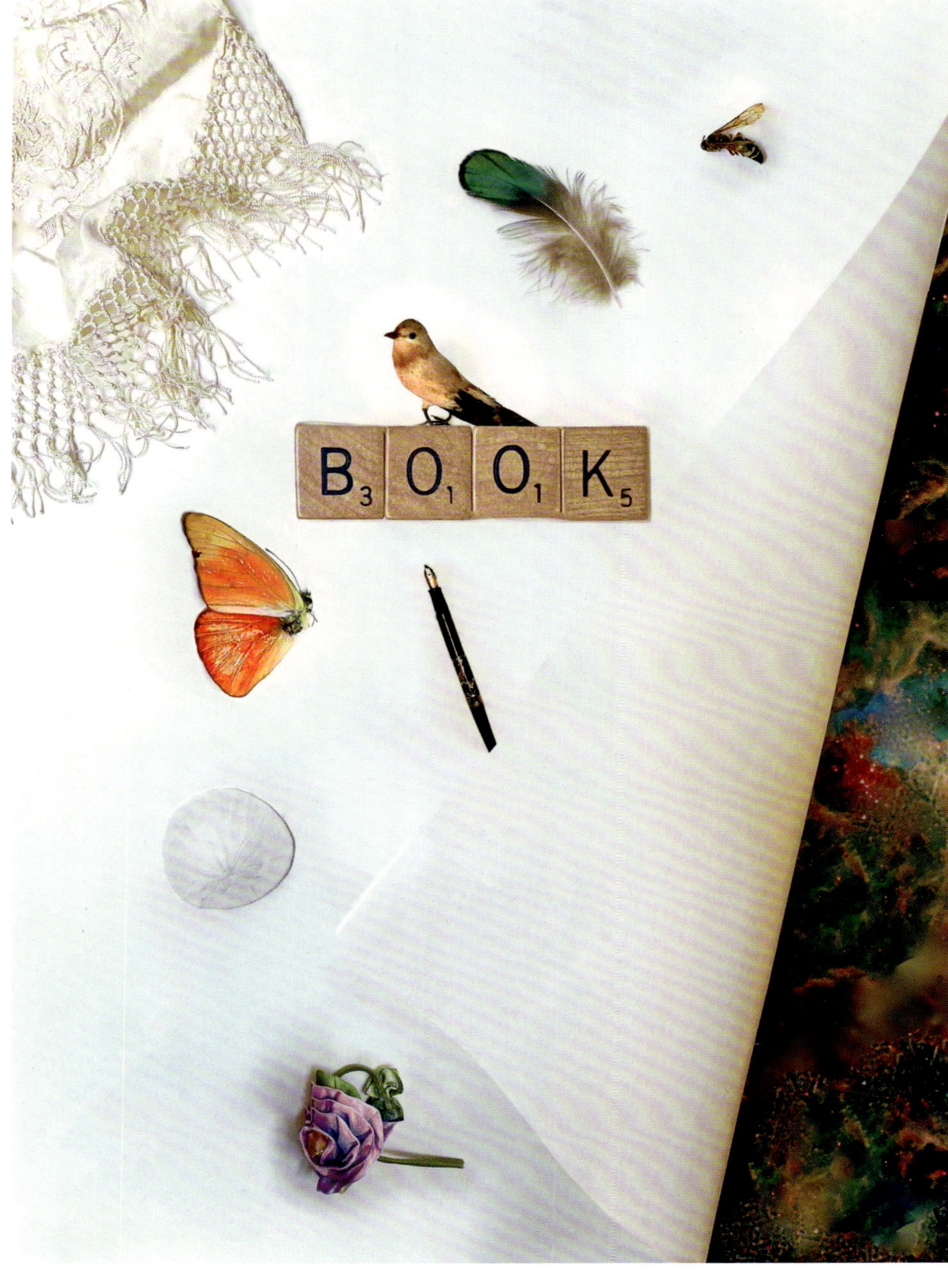
B3 O1 O1 K5

FOREWORD

From the very first illustration *Complements: eloquence of small objects* is a mélange of juxtapositions, contrasts, clashes, and harmonies. There is humor and insight at every turn.

I was struck by what an imaginative and powerful piece of work it is. I originally saw many of the photos on, where else, Facebook. They were taken on the iPhone and posted over a year as individual images, almost in real time as they were produced. On their own the photographs are original and stunning, but by convening them in one place, and pairing them like couples at a dance, Patricia Smith has conjured up an artistic *tour de force*.

She told me that *Complements* "is not about technique, though most of the photographs required more or less complex set-ups, some ridiculous looking contraptions with teacups attached to wires hanging from out-of-view clothes hangers, a bra hanging from a branch nailed to the wall, a butterfly perched on a skull of feathers. Because I prefer naturally lit images, they needed to be moved as the light coming through the windows changed." I can only imagine her scrambling around to catch the last rays before the sun set. As a fellow photographer, I know the feeling. Life for us is the pursuit of the right light and moment.

The text for the photos weaves a magical web that melds perfectly with the images, telling their stories and revealing their secrets. The narrative between words and pictures reunites twins separated at birth.

Patricia said, "The images came easily to me. Some of them like the fish in the bowl, the mouse in the maze, the bull's horn through the wallpaper, and the flowers hanging from the clothesline materialized unsummoned as complete images, and I simply brought the objects together." In other words, when Michelangelo was asked how he created one of his finest masterpieces, he supposedly answered, "It's easy. You chip away all the marble that doesn't look like David." I'm sure that's apocryphal, but it is a valid observation of an artistic mind that creates something out of nothing.

Patricia has sculpted a unique place for herself in the world of fine art. She said, "Since earliest childhood I have searched to find, reveal, convey what I sense beyond the tangible, and I ponder why we all don't search for that incessantly. We live on a thin sheet of dimensions, time, and physicality as though that is all there is. It confounds and irritates me. I want the photographs to hone and enlarge the viewer's perspective. How is it that objects stimulate emotions, thoughts, and memories inside us? What is the nature of that language and how do we become fluent in it? And why, when objects are juxtaposed, do our emotions, thoughts, and memories become more complex, become a storyline—more than the sum of their parts?"

In my world, and I describe myself as an old-fashioned news photographer, my mission is to accurately document the truth. Patricia's reality is one of her own creation and a product of her vivid curiosity. She is driven to find what is around her that is beyond the obvious. She throws things and possibilities in the air to see where they land. In this cosmic toss of the dice, Patricia has rolled a winner.

David Hume Kennerly
Pulitzer Prize Winner, Former Chief White House Photographer

Photographs capture light's creations as wisps of forever.

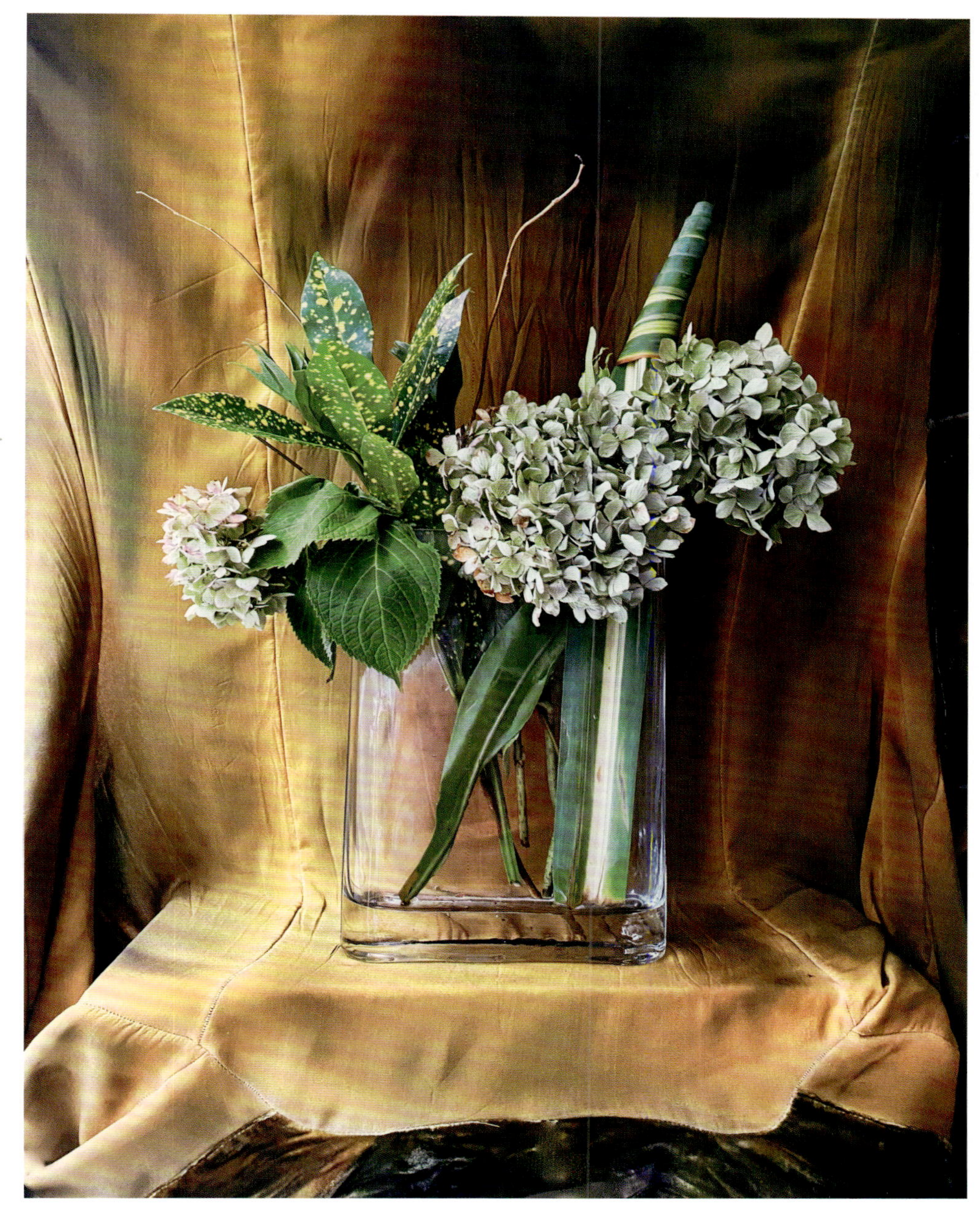

Things that create of each other more than the sum of their parts

Objects have presence, in form and meaning. Their physical qualities—shape, color, smell, texture, assigned use, and condition—evoke intangible qualities of mood, memory, longing, intent, joy, injury, and awe in the viewer. Objects hold the stuff of stories.

Set in relationship to each other, objects are complements that entwine the potential of their separate stories into larger stories—more complex, nuanced, intimate, intriguing. These intangible qualities bounce off each other, tease each other, threaten each other, reveal a glory in each other—and in the mysterious processes of imagination and metaphor, we viewers can be pulled through portals to where spoken and written language have no say. Only intangibles can reveal intangibles.

Wordless metaphors and allusions can open a vault of original knowledge inside us, a familiarity, a remembering that alludes to the largest story. What is beyond objects?

As a photographer, I have always received, even been beset by, visions that take me further and further into exploring the "I AM" beyond time and space. My camera is a scalpel, retriever, and lover.

I work with objects.

Do they give me life, or do I give them life?

Patricia Z. Smith

Her heart quickened as the pull of the Great Mystery grew.
How wondrous it must be to be so strong! Cheese? A moon of her own?

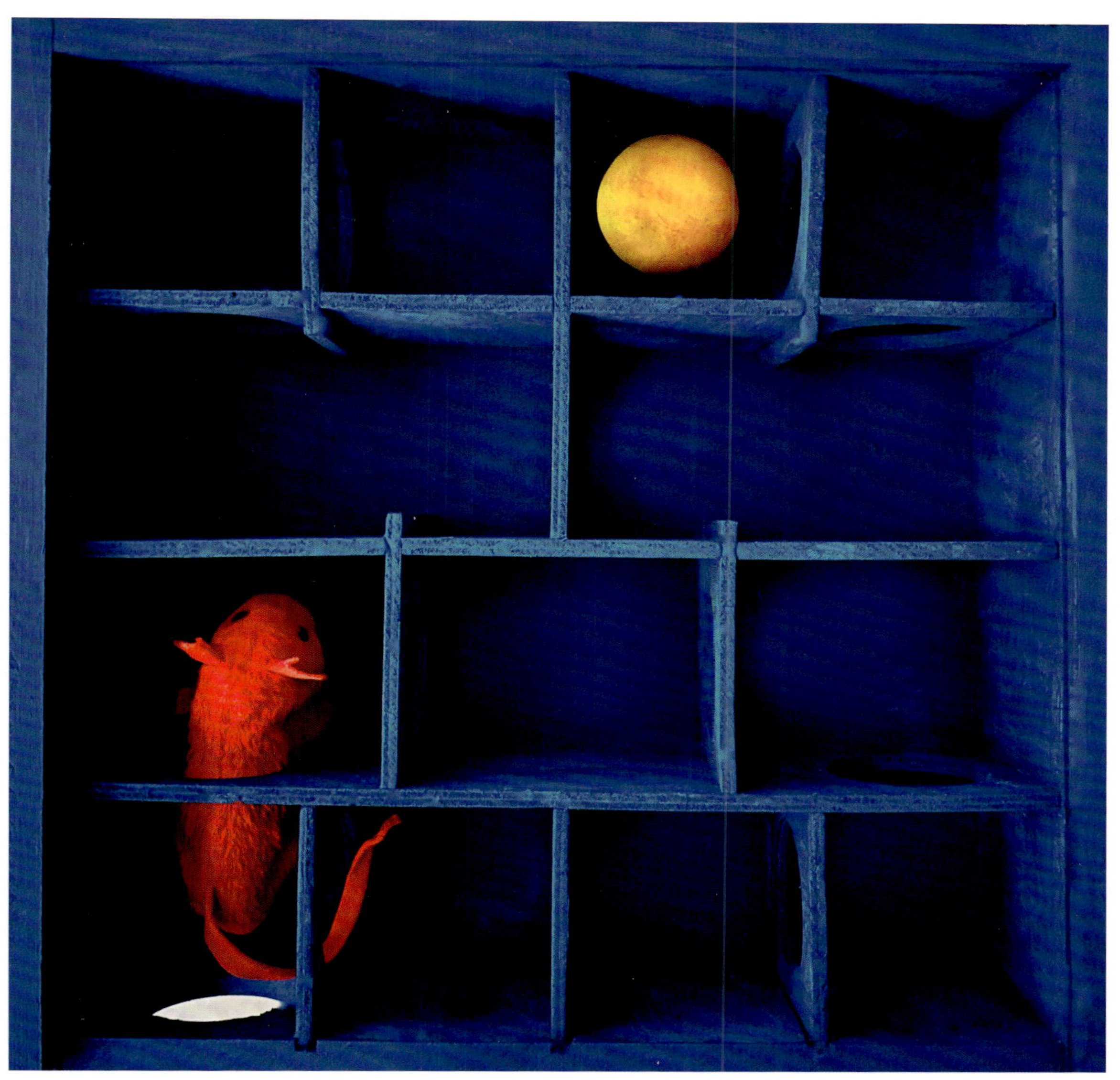

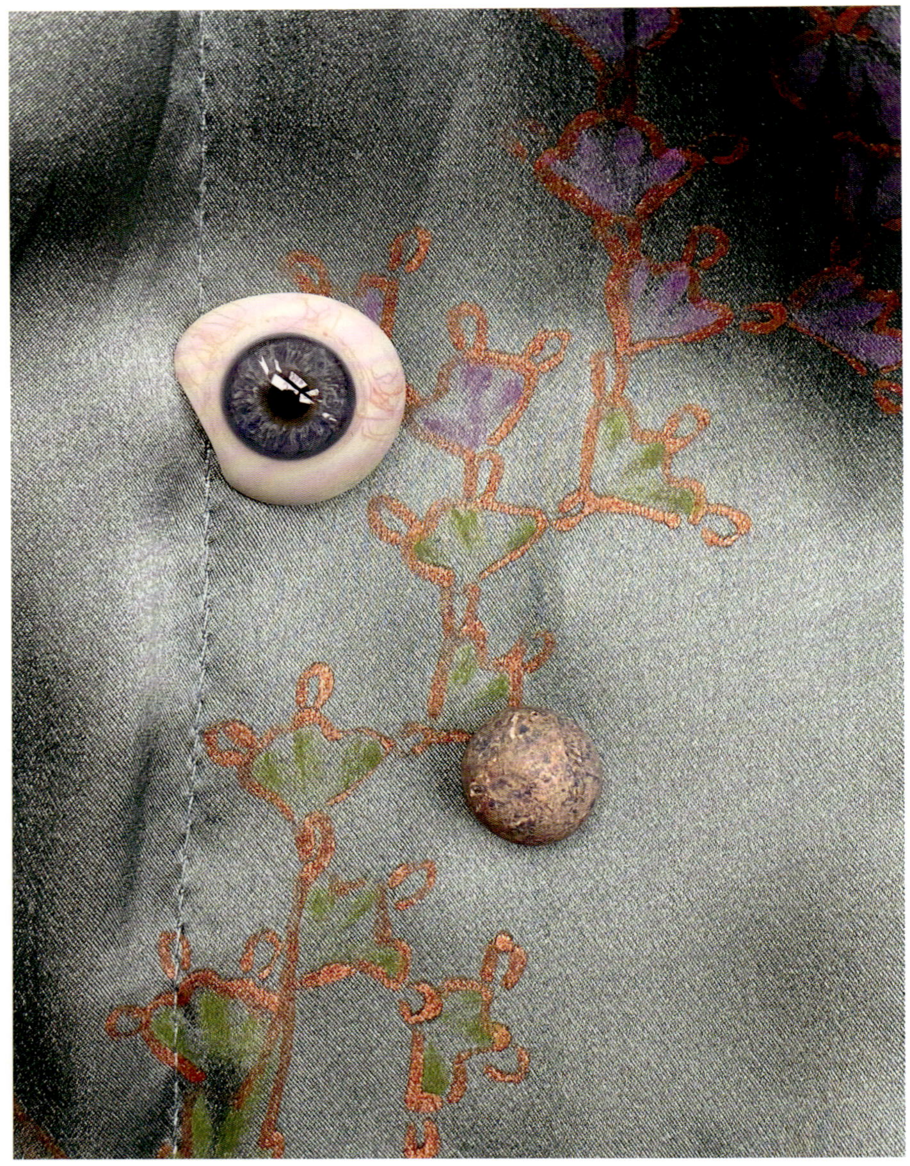

You believe I am innocuous, a glass trick, inert as a handmade marble, but you are wrong. I am looking at you, and I make you see what I see.

—glass eye, German, made after WWI

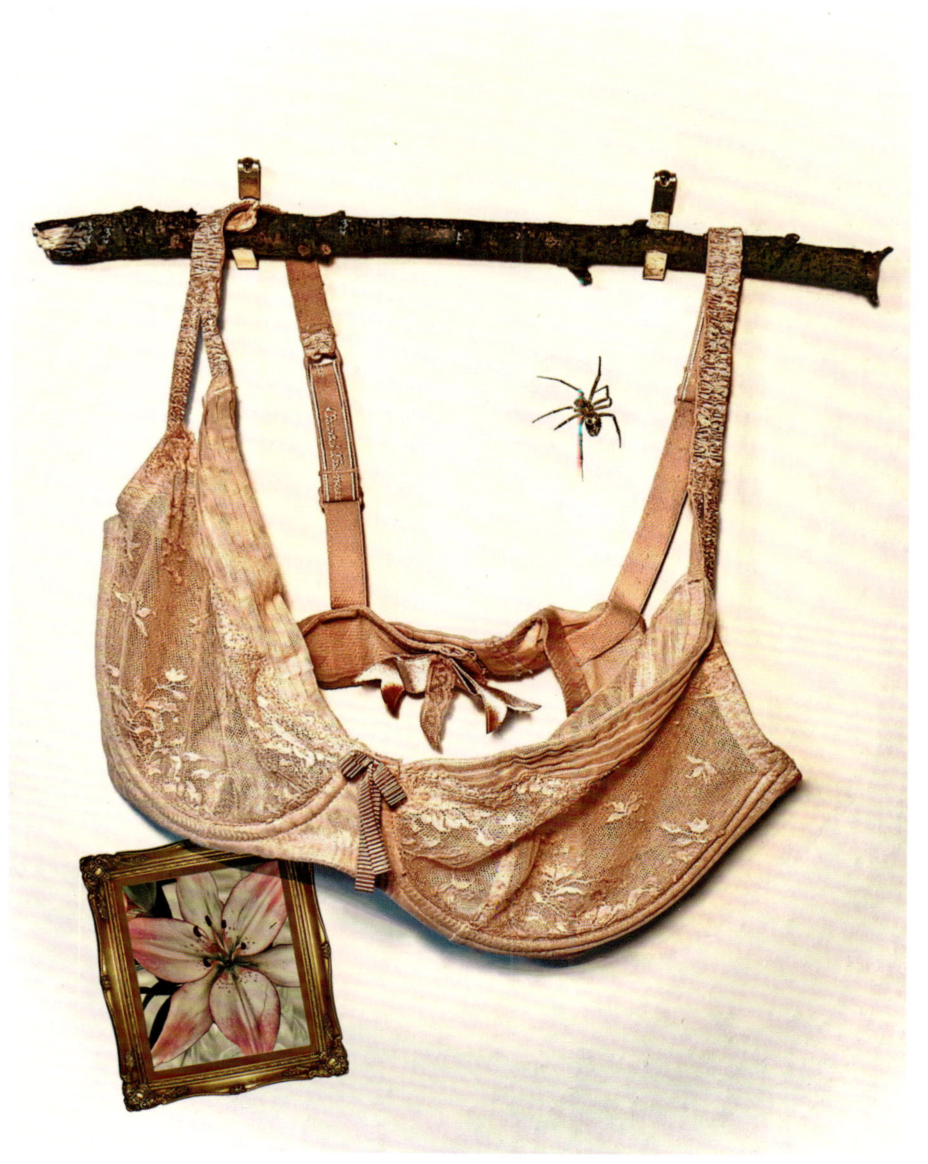

Bra on a branch, flower in a frame, a spider. . .hmmm?

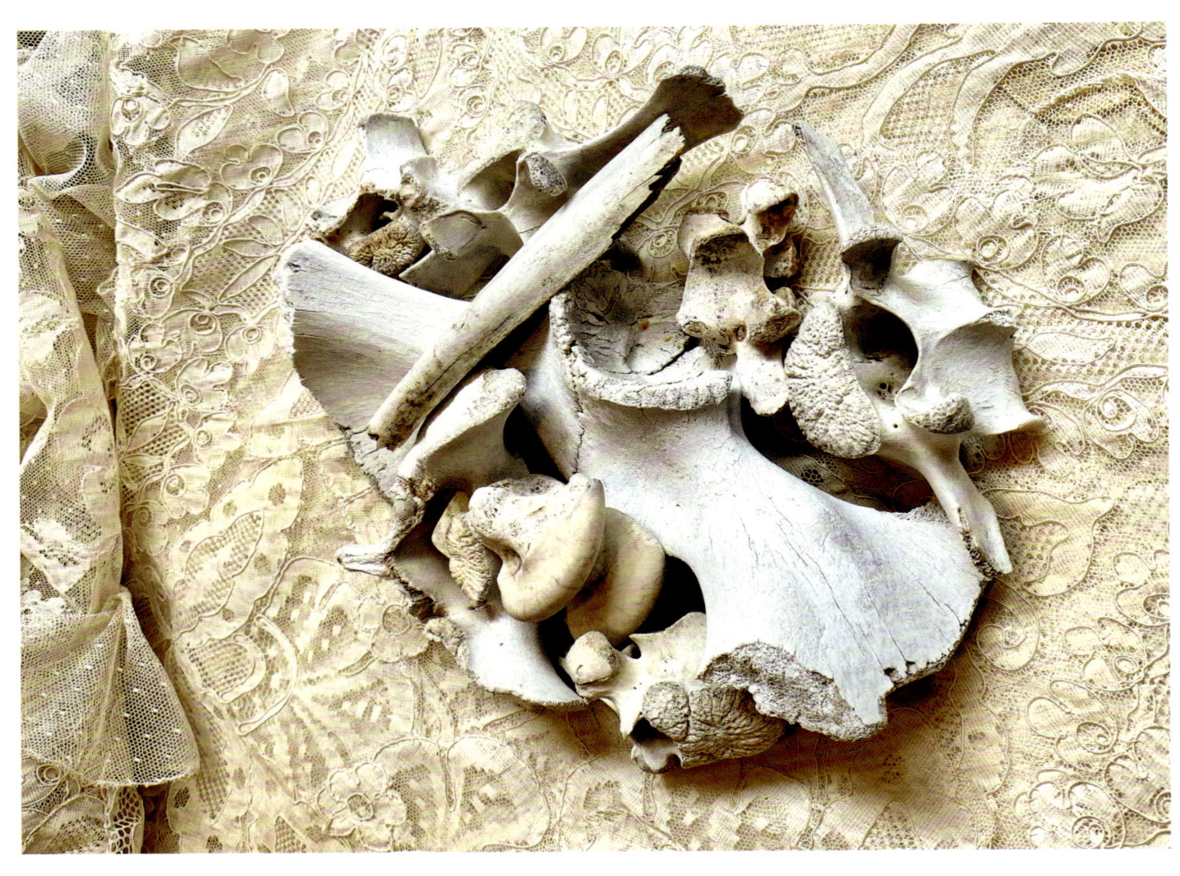

Bones—elegant detritus—collapse time and hold secrets. So does my lace wedding cloak.

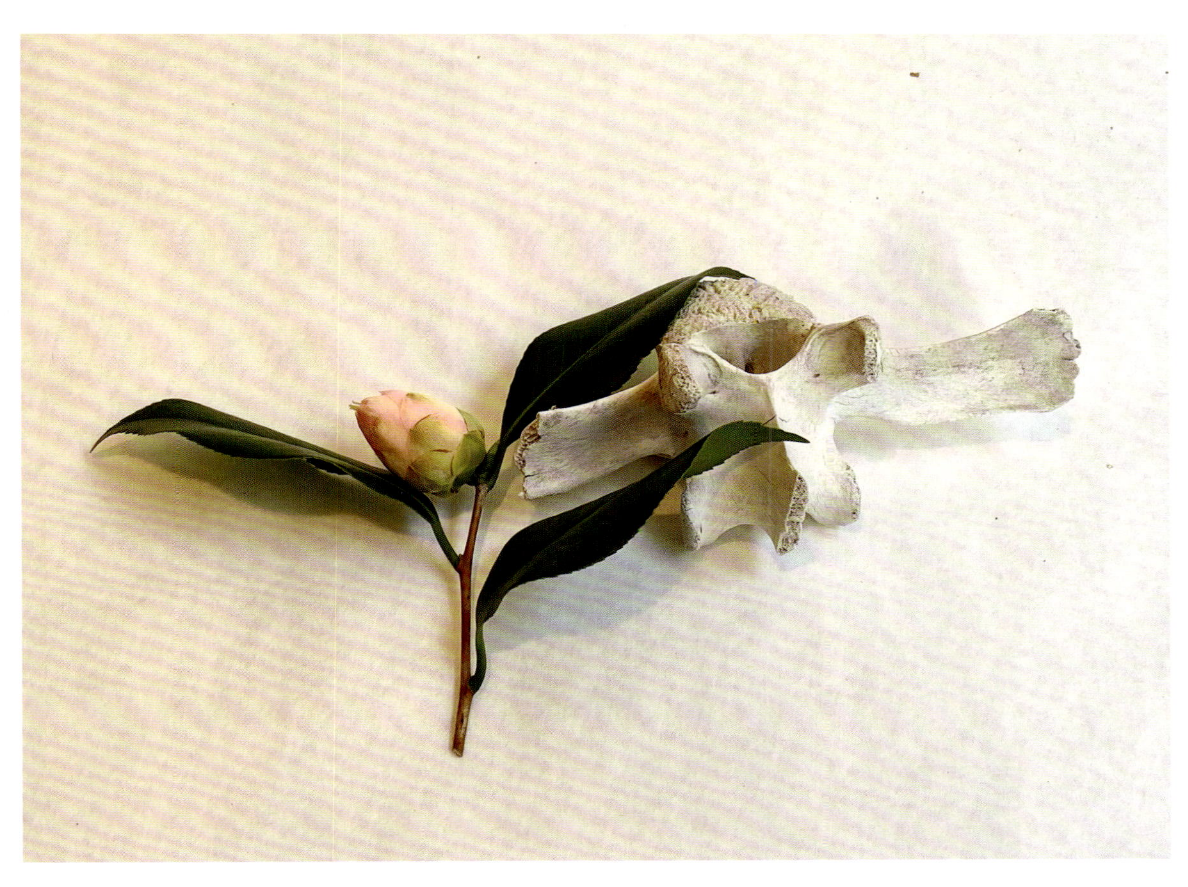

I heard a bird chirp, filled with hope.

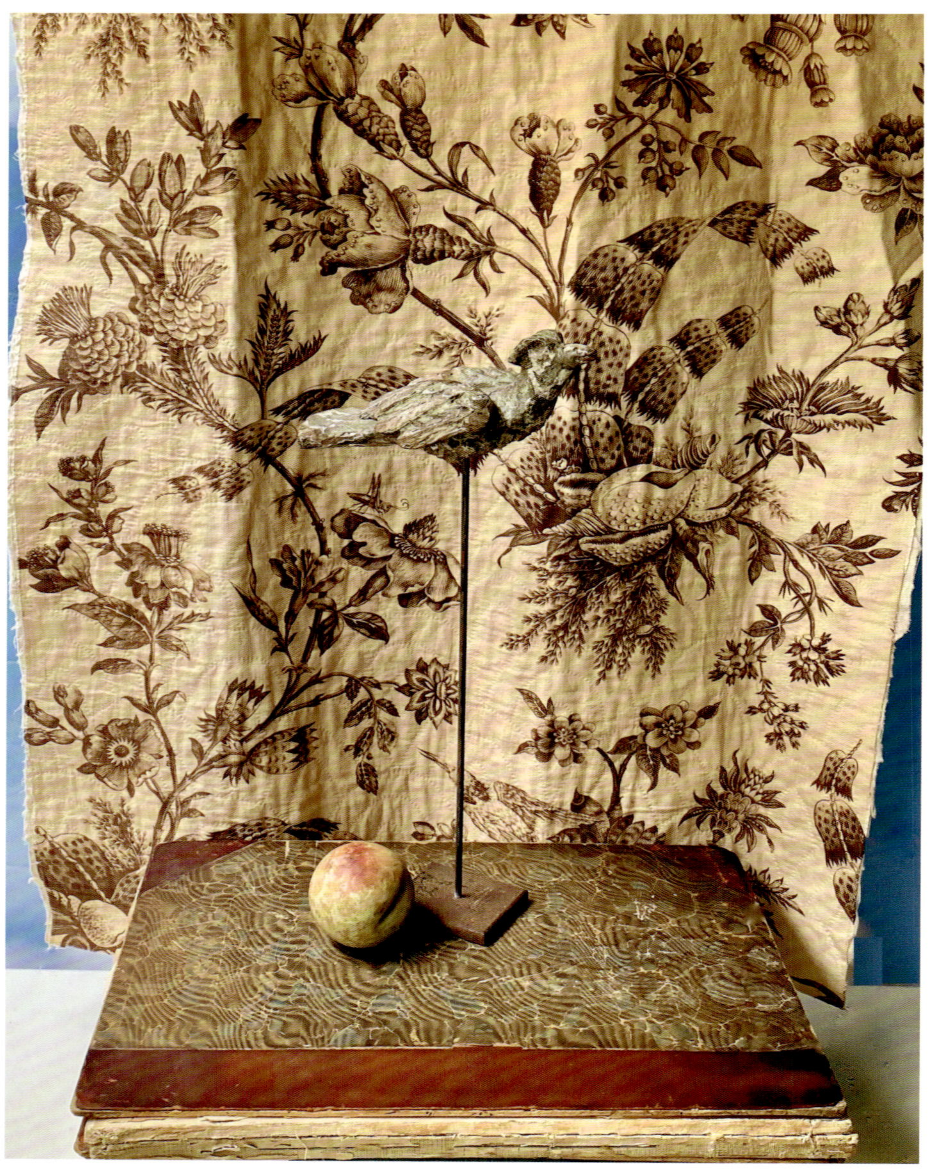

What glory this? Fabric printed by copperplate c.1810 near Versailles, bird carved of wood in Provence, catalog of architectural details, stone peach found in Paris.

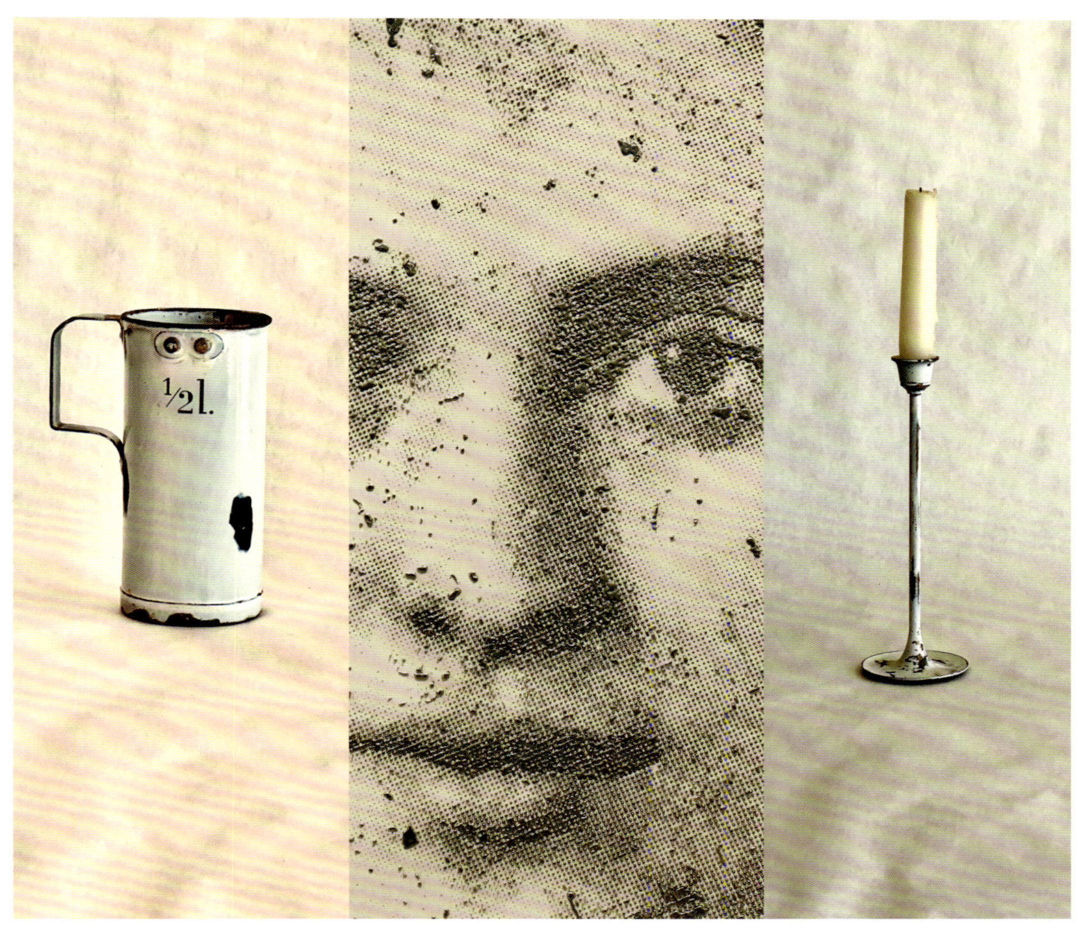

At dusk she often walked to the woods at the edge of the lawn
where she pressed her body into the oak tree until she bruised.

—musing on Emily D.

Stop trying to make sense of things!

—page 259, Encyclopedia of Irrationalities

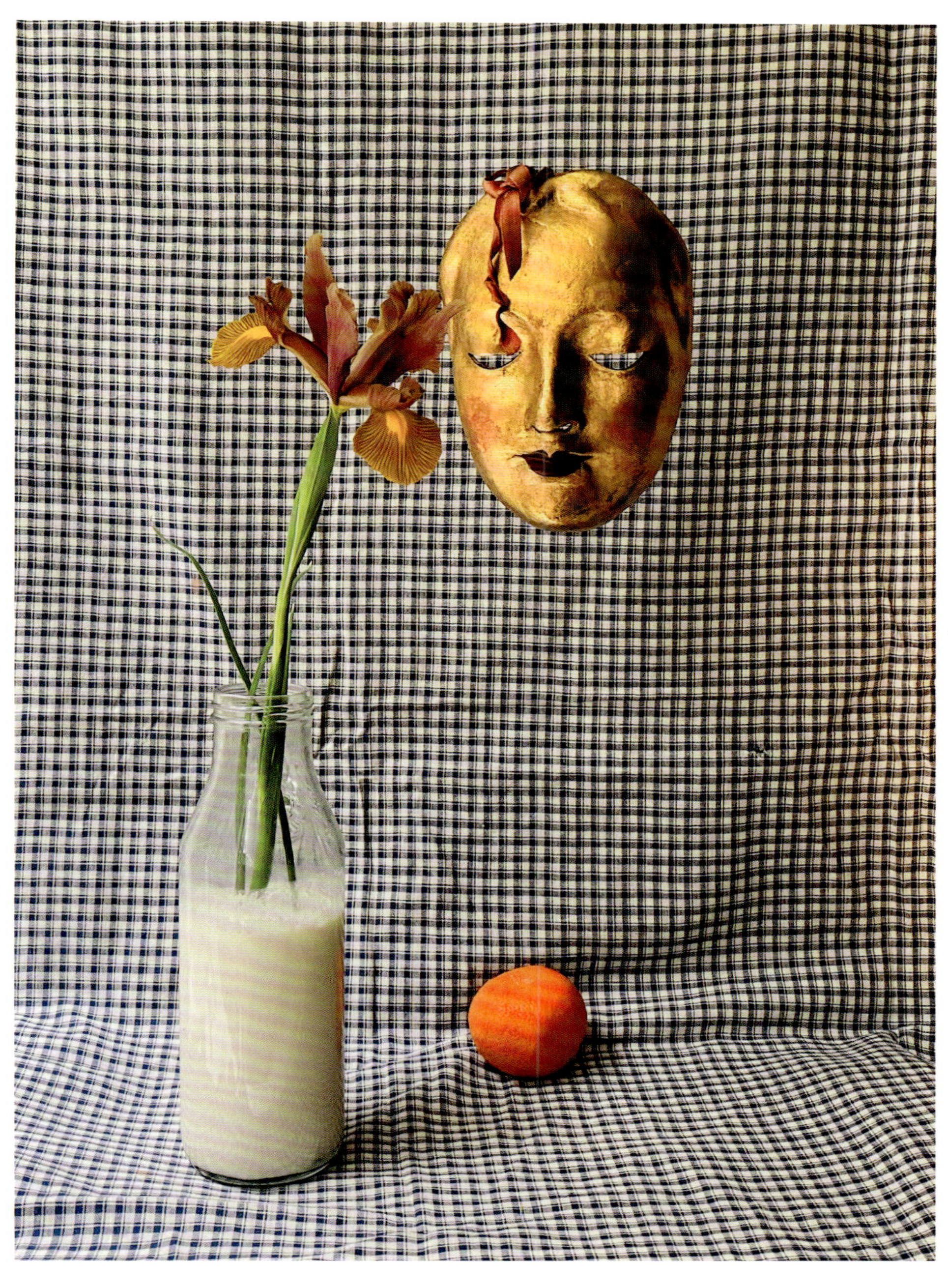

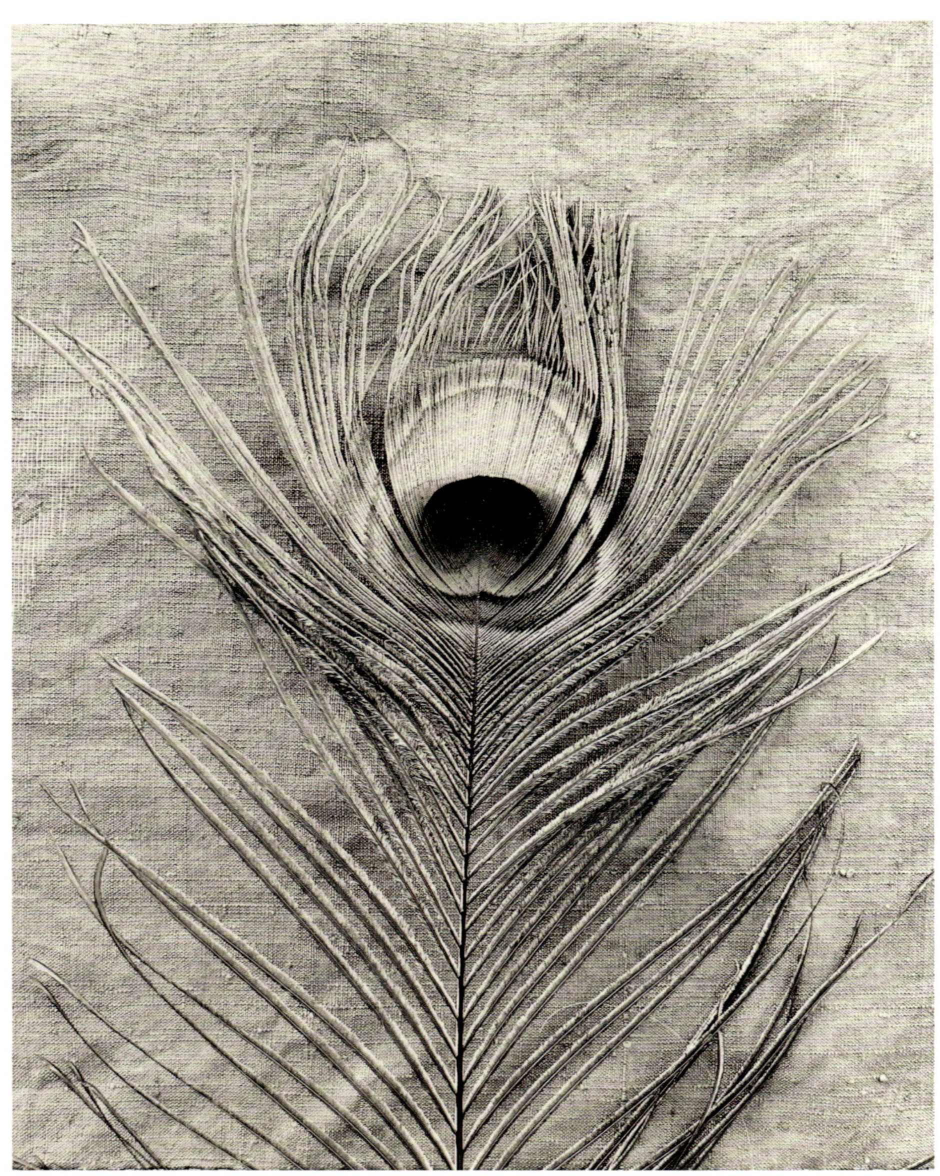

A feather's touch can break you open.

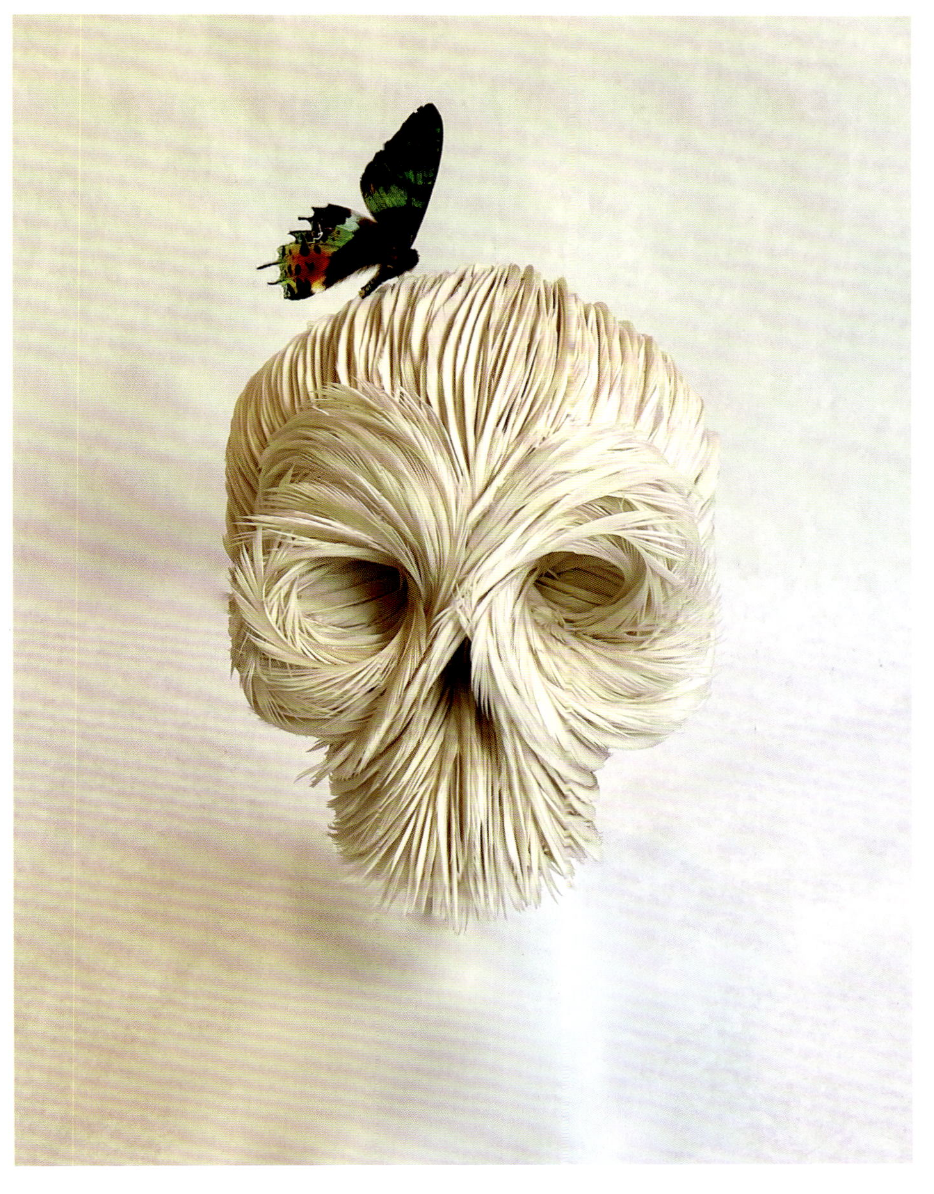

It's so light.

—Mirose, *resin and goose feathers, by Laurence Le Constant, 2012*

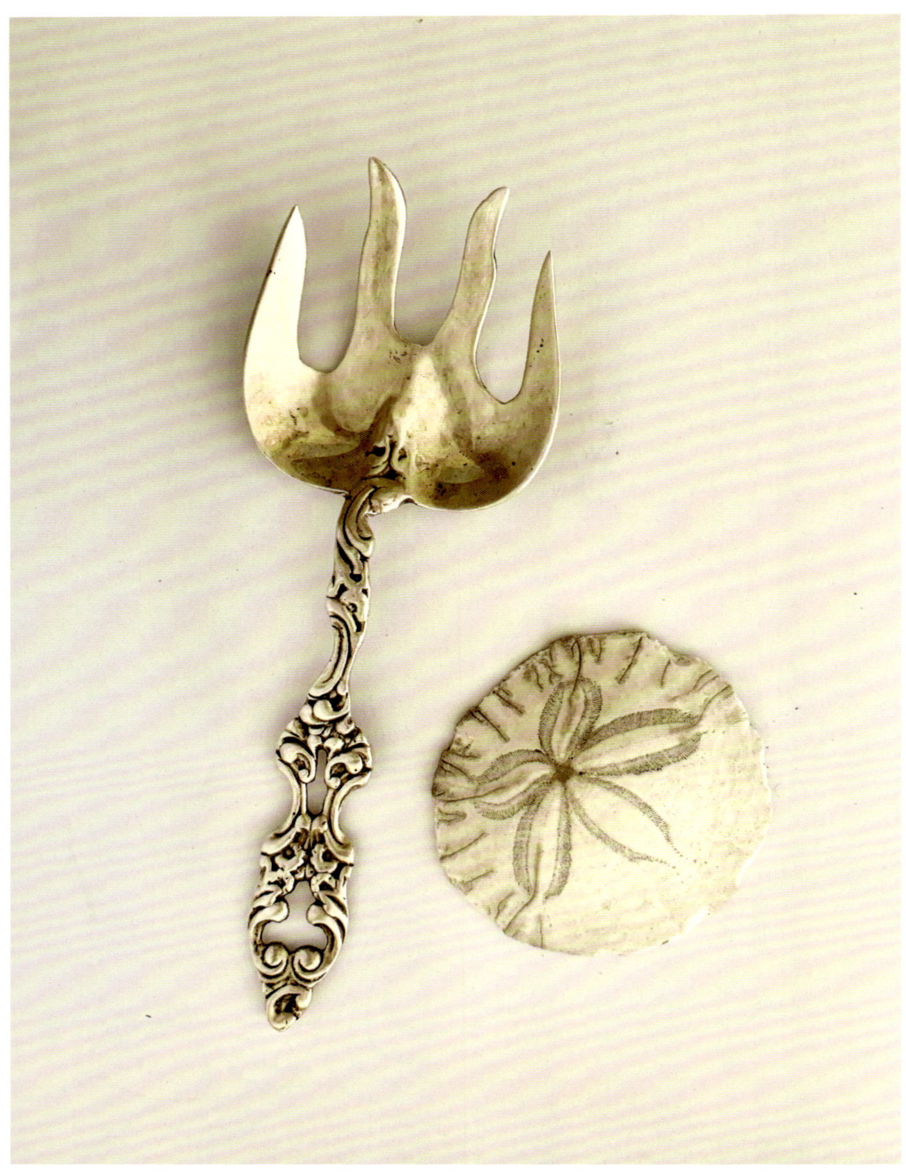

Serenity cannot be imposed. Yet, with grace, sometimes it reveals itself through your hands.

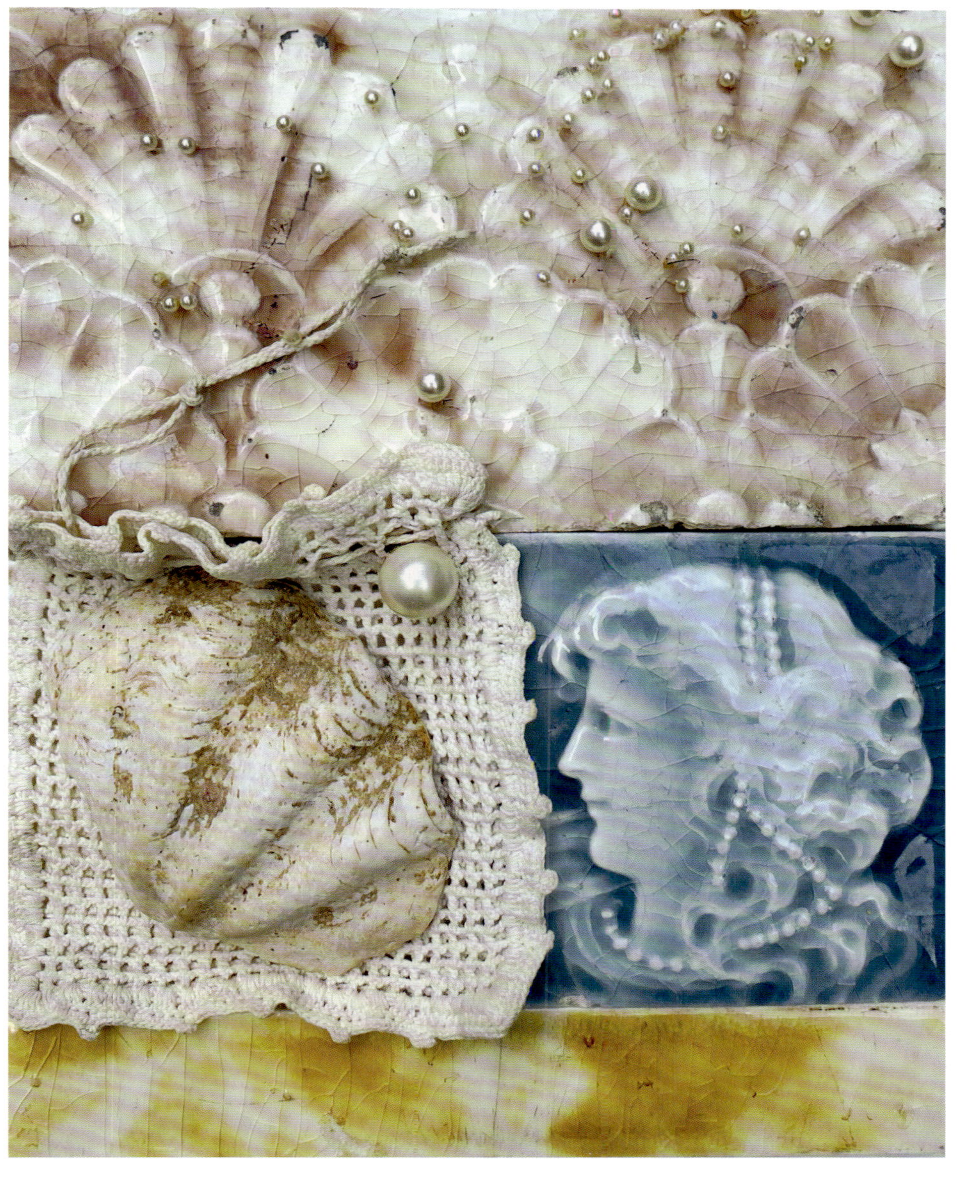

She wore pearls in her hair when he was on his sea voyages, believing it would strengthen her devotion. Time passed slowly, and she was often tempted.

Find the netsuke of stag's antler carved into mushrooms on a fir leaf. Hold it, feel its smoothness. Japanese, Edo Period, 19th century. Find the clam-like brachiopod. Feel the ocean in it. Tennessee, Middle Jurassic, 150–180 million years ago.

—page 423, Encyclopedia of Irrationalities

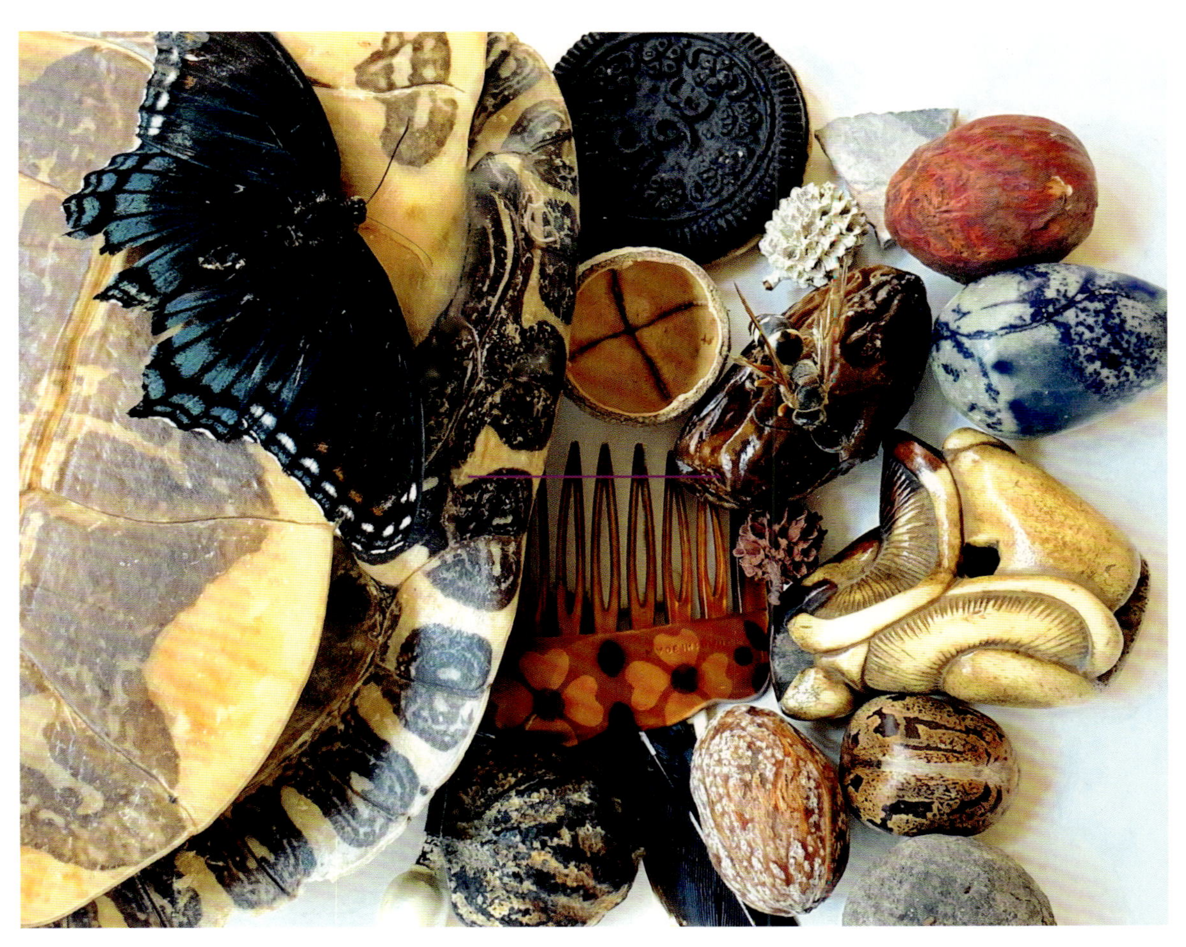

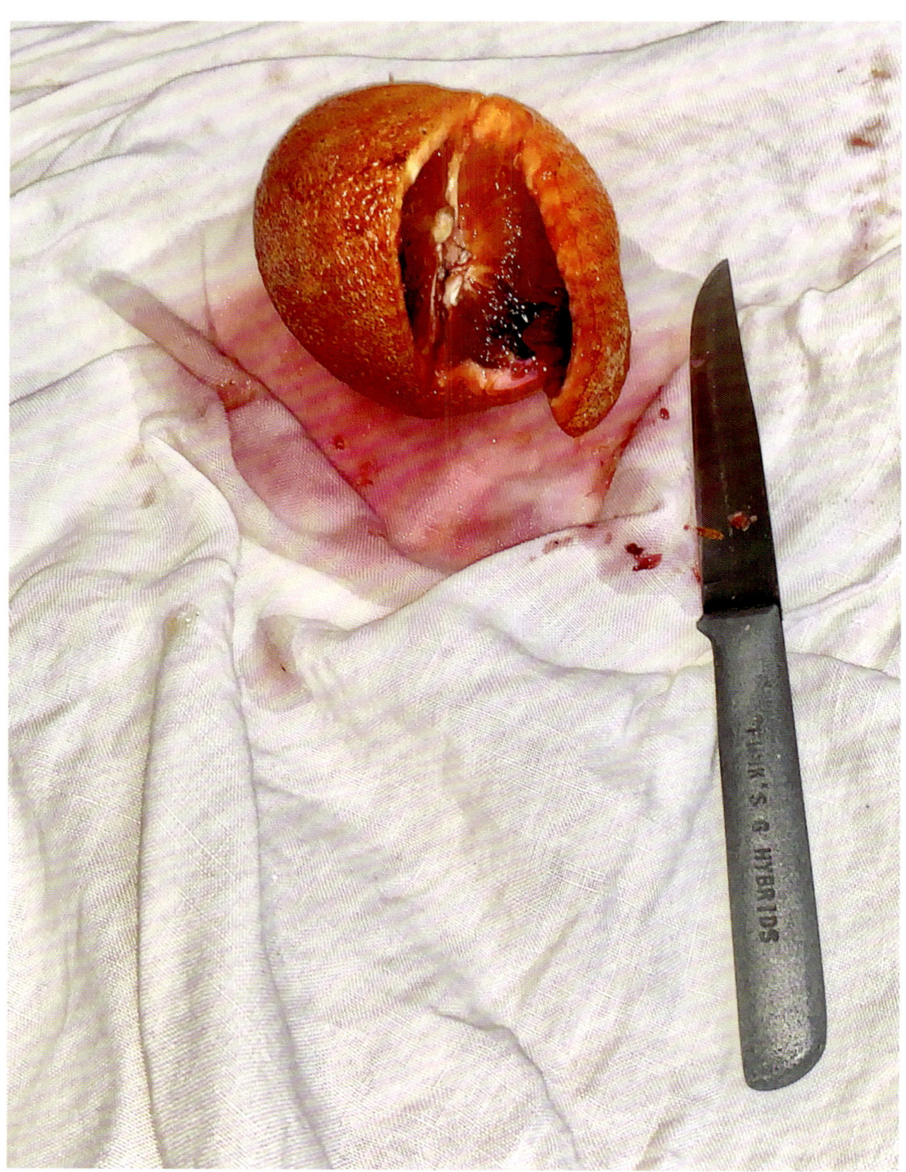

He stepped cautiously through the briars and rusty barbed wire,
but he didn't see the knife until it sliced through his shoe to his foot.
In seconds he would be blasted to smithereens like his comrades...

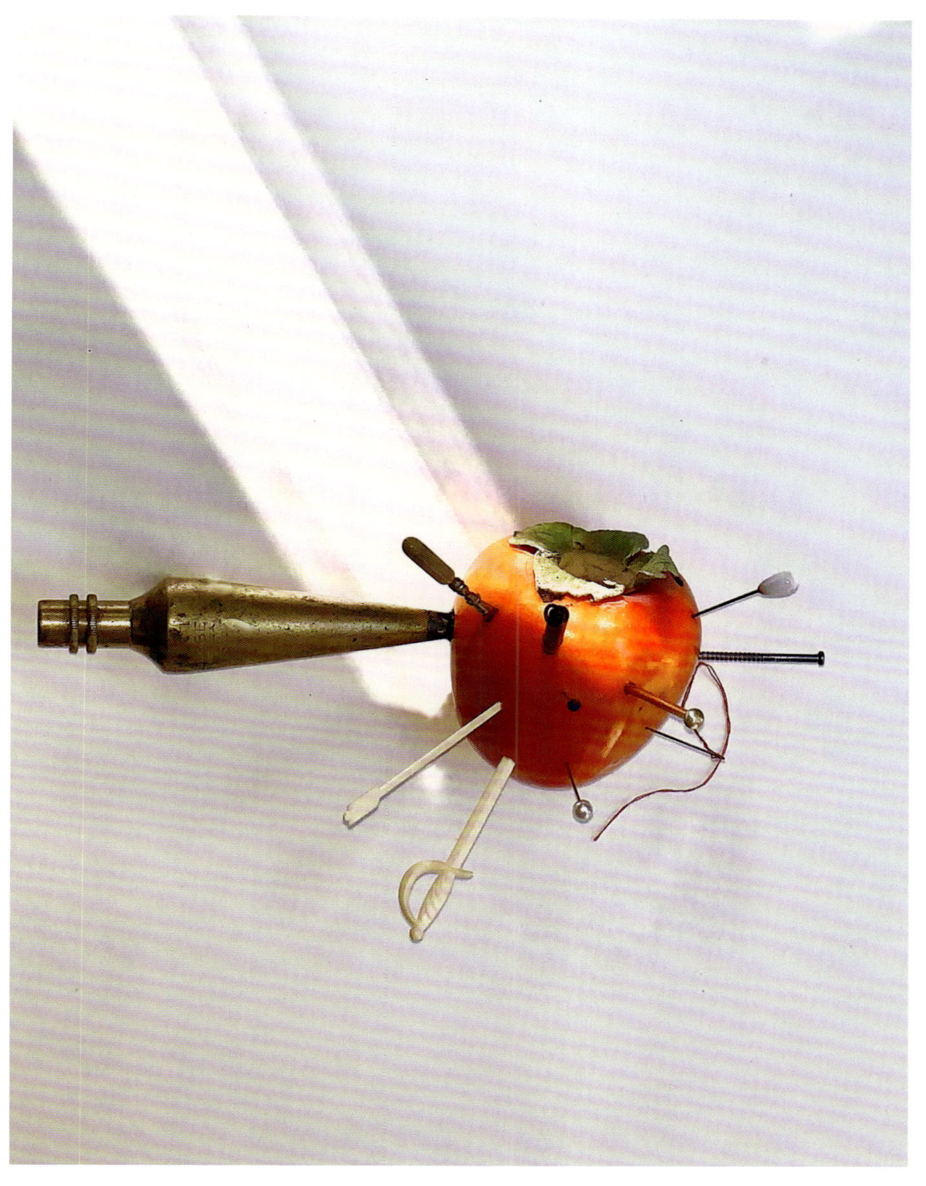

. . .but the blast did not come as destruction but as a shaft of light through the trees overhead.
He was pierced, wounded, but he was home, returned to the Iowa homestead.
It was a knife like those his father gave farmers when he sold them hybrid seed corn.

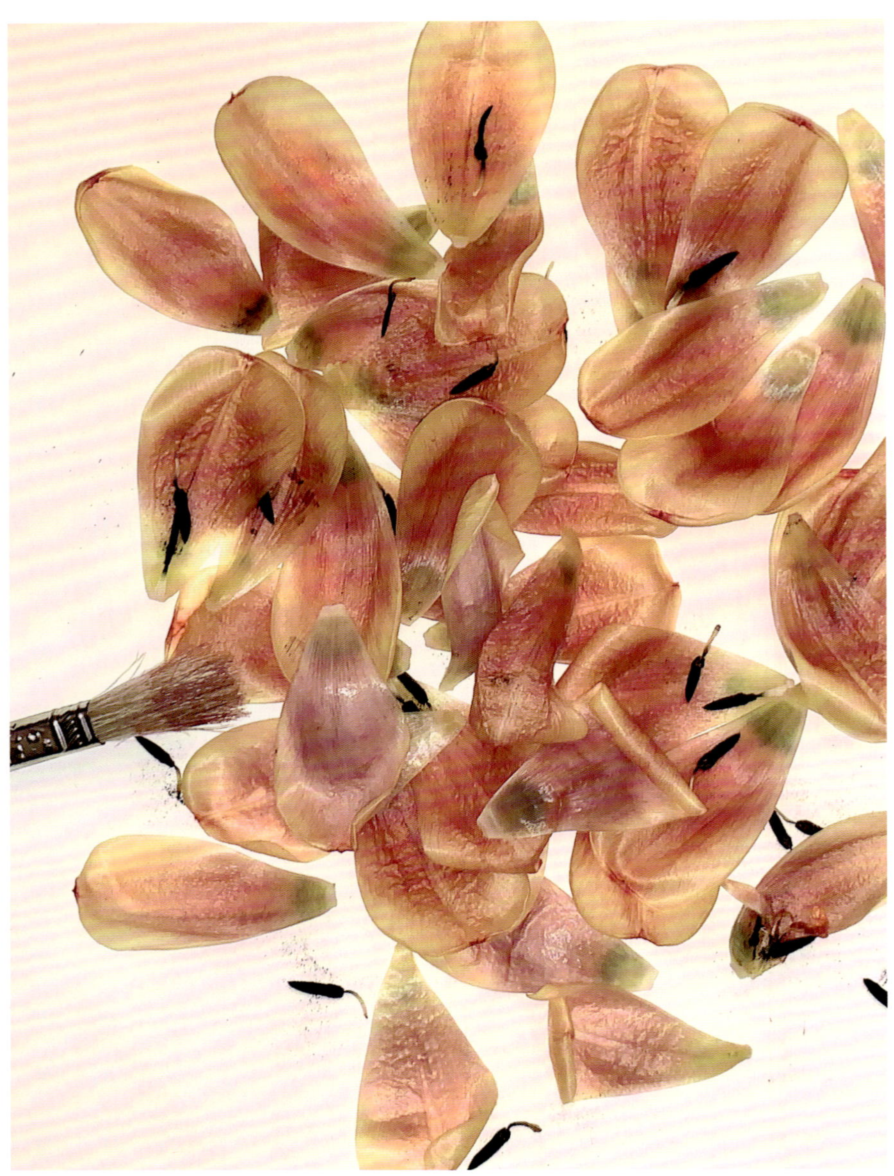

As he fell to his knees he saw flowers beyond the briars.
He had a choice. He could chose flowers instead of bombs.

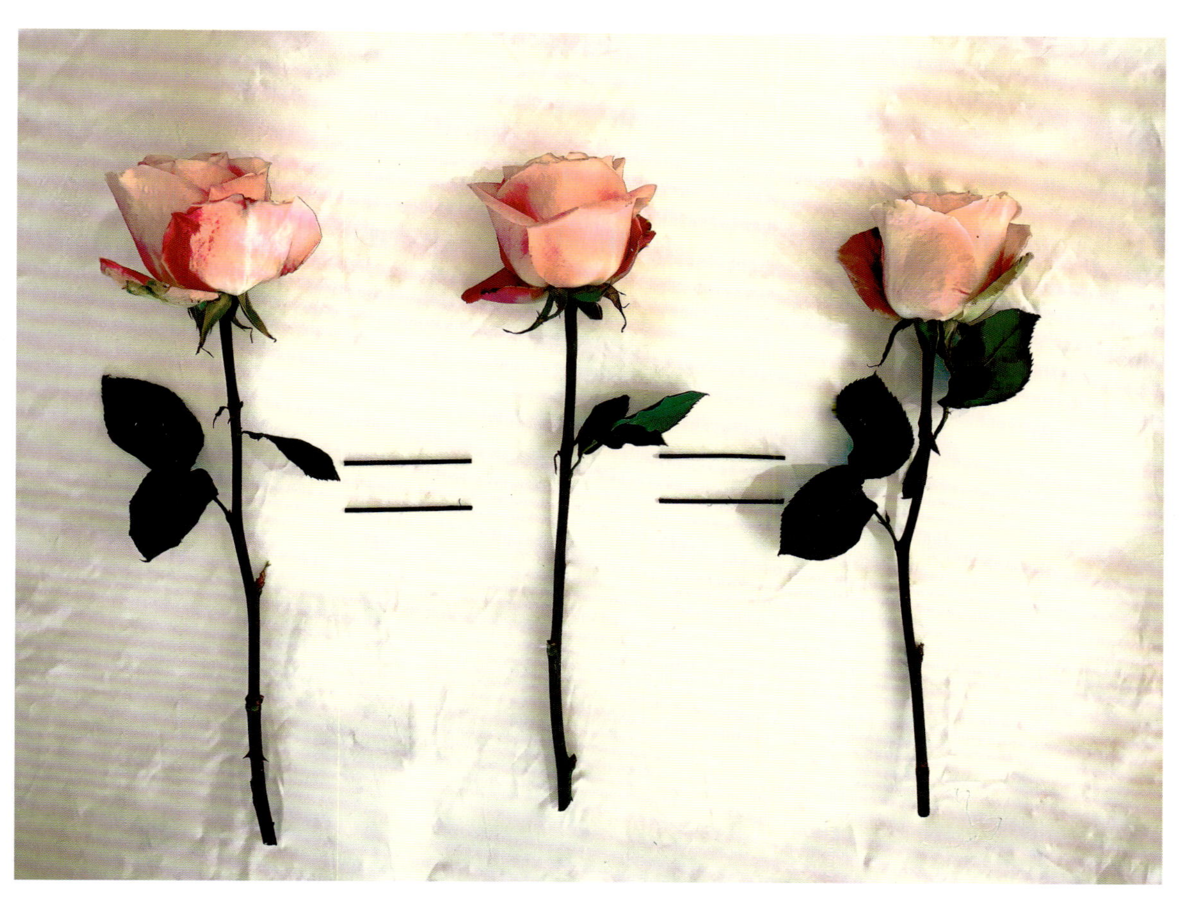

A rose is a rose is a rose.

—Gertrude Stein, straight up absurdist poet

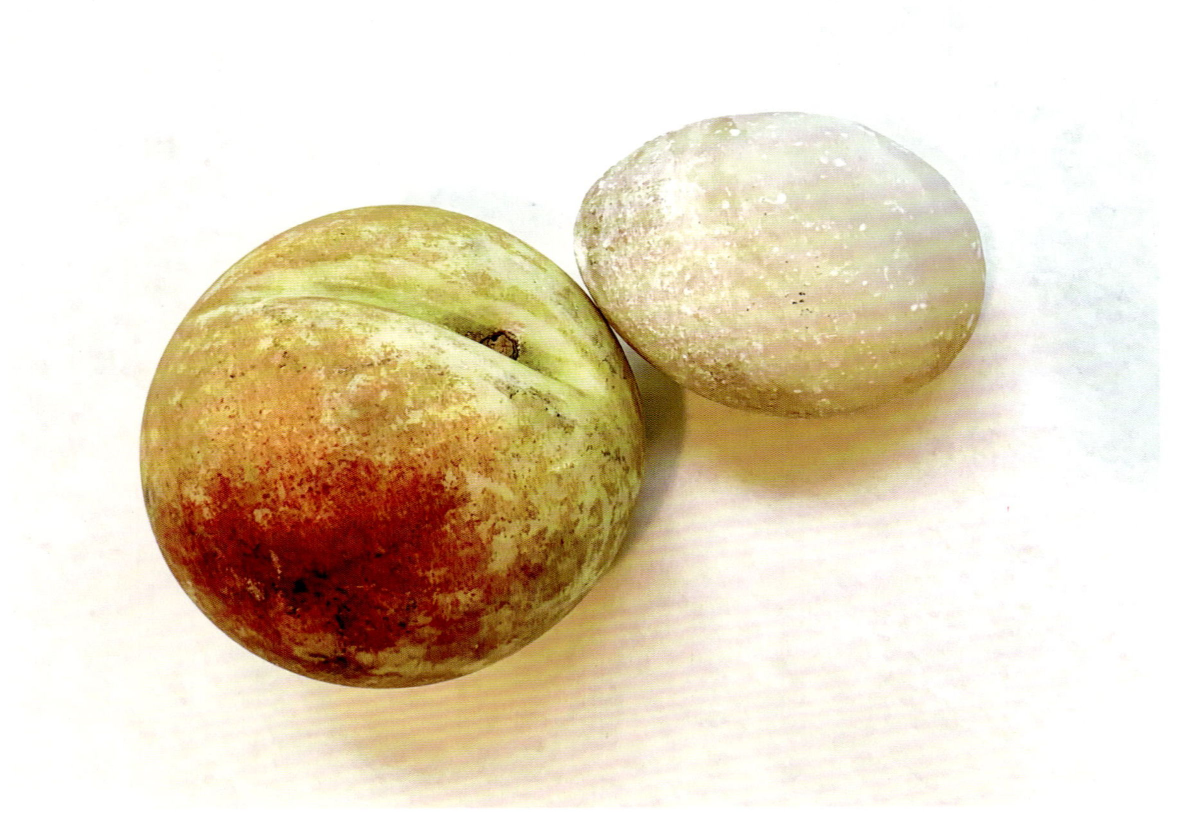

The stones kissed each other, tasted each other's past—homes of French aristocrats and a riverbed in New Mexico.

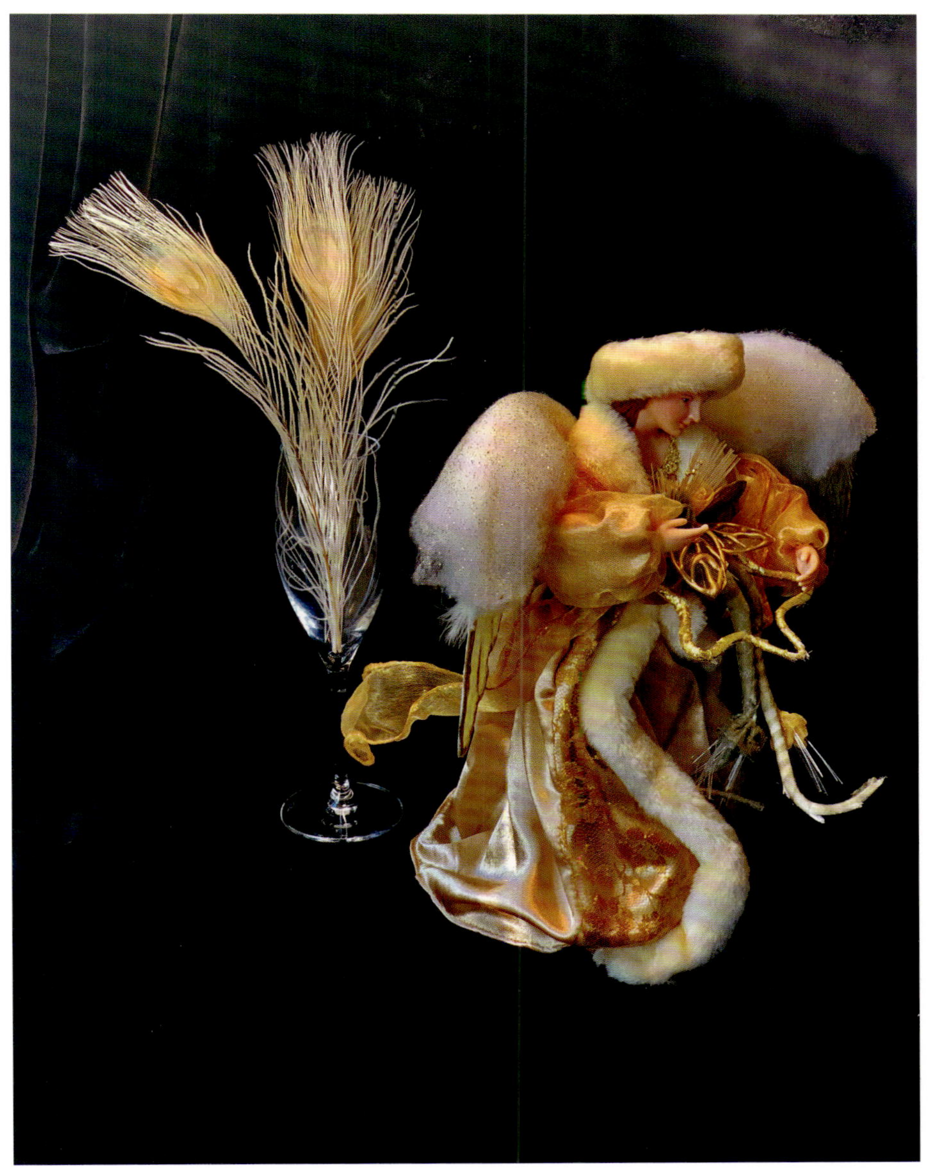

The angel lowered her wings and left the stage with only fragile hope we would remember her, but some of us have and long for her return —or we long for something, but don't know what it is.

"It's my secret," said God, "like when the caterpillar is liquid before becoming a butterfly."

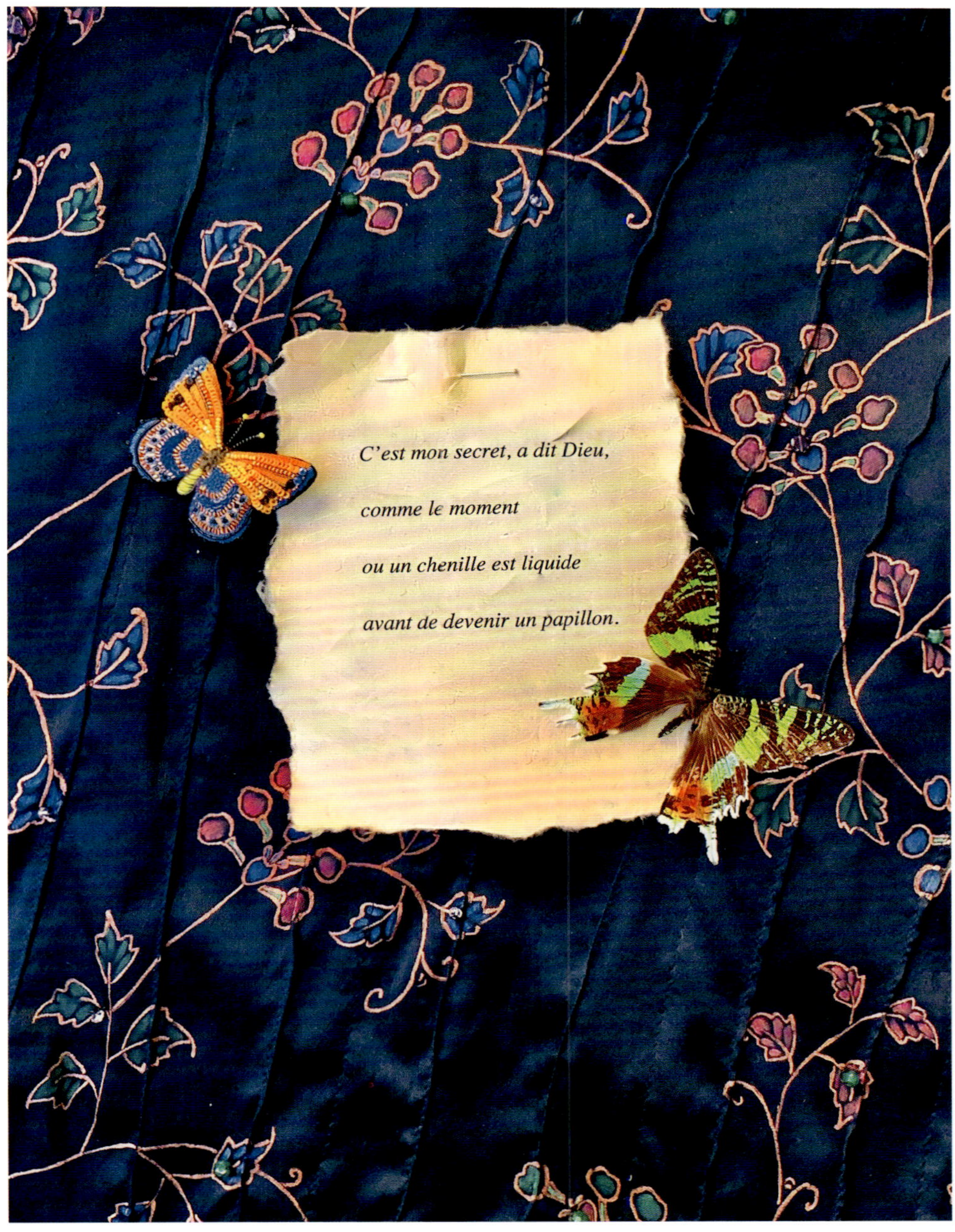
C'est mon secret, a dit Dieu,
comme le moment
ou un chenille est liquide
avant de devenir un papillon.

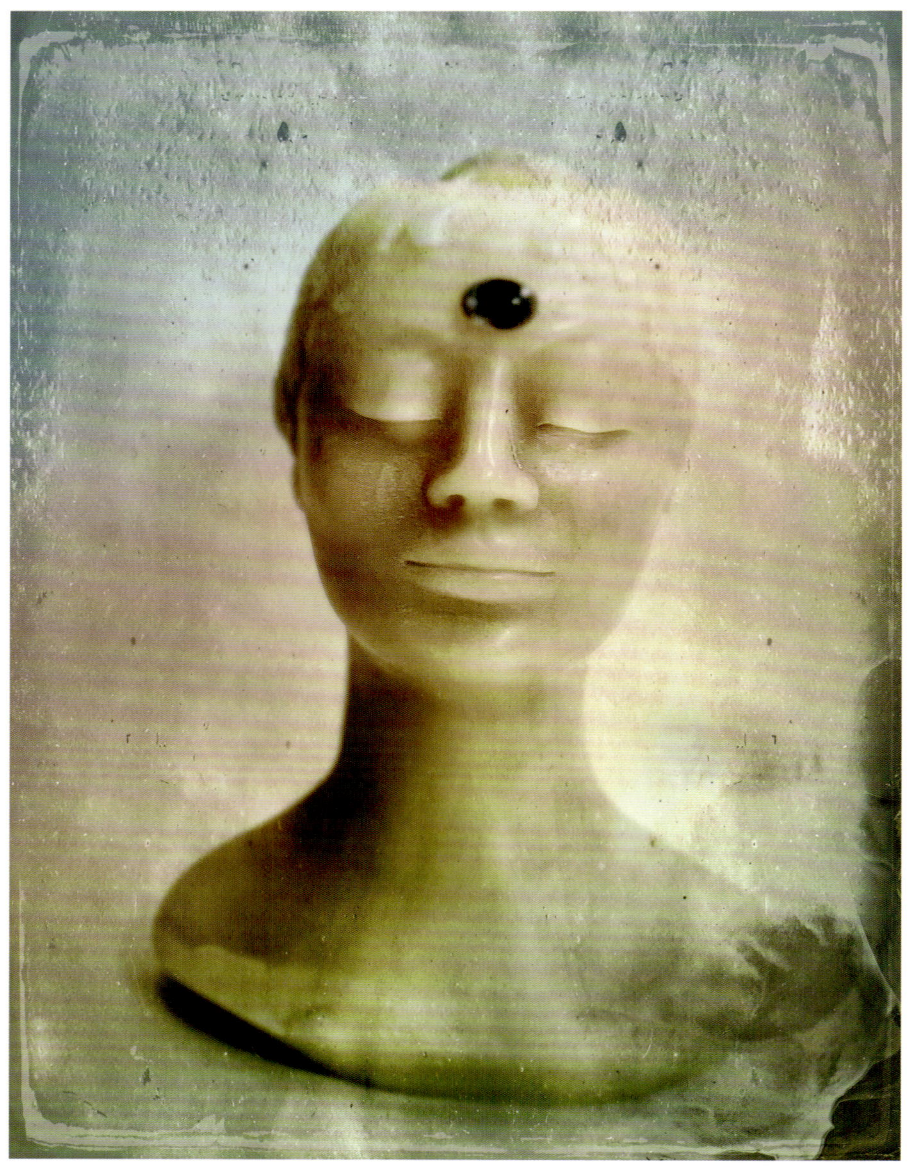

Bliss is a comet. First fire, then a tail, then you never forget.

—wax candle sculpture by Beatrix Ost, 2007

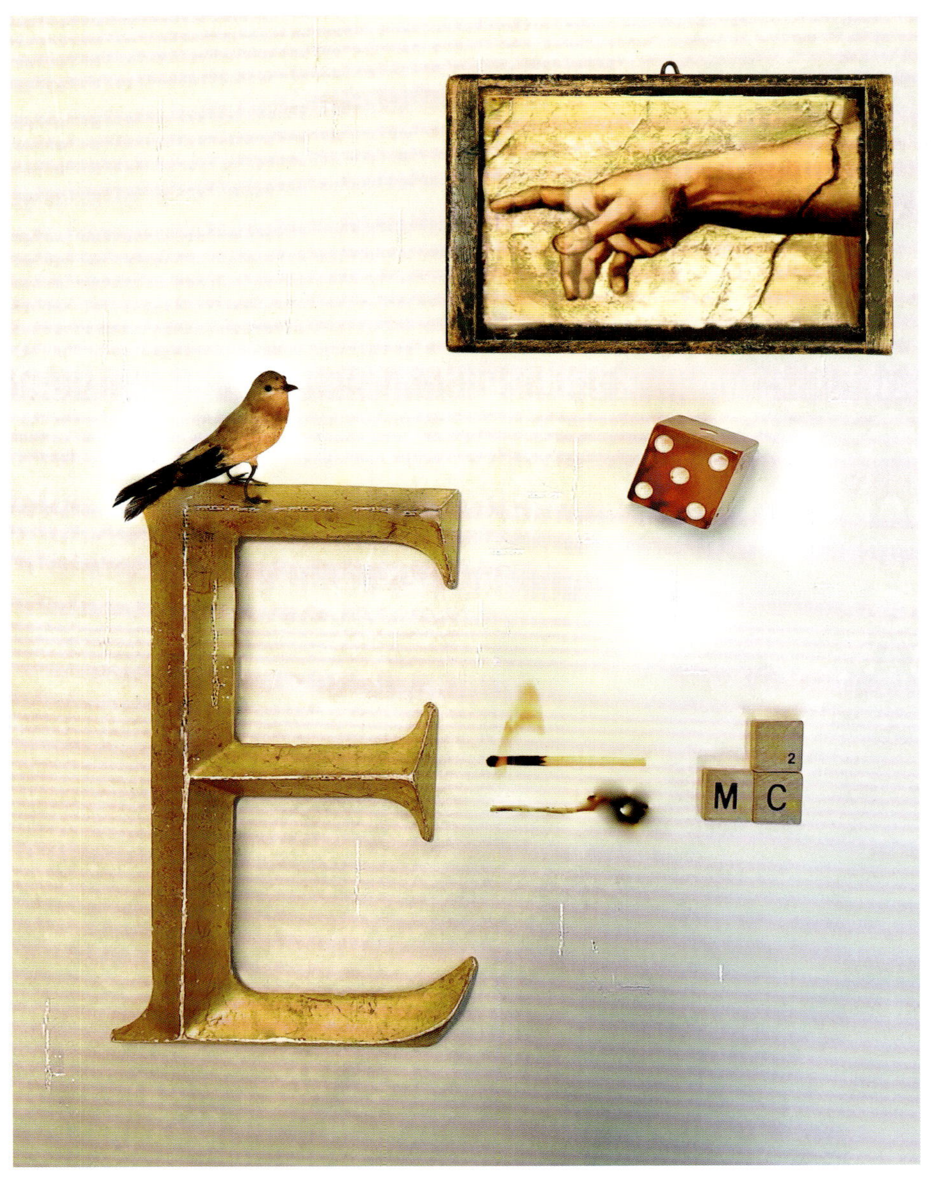

God does not play dice. Wanna bet?

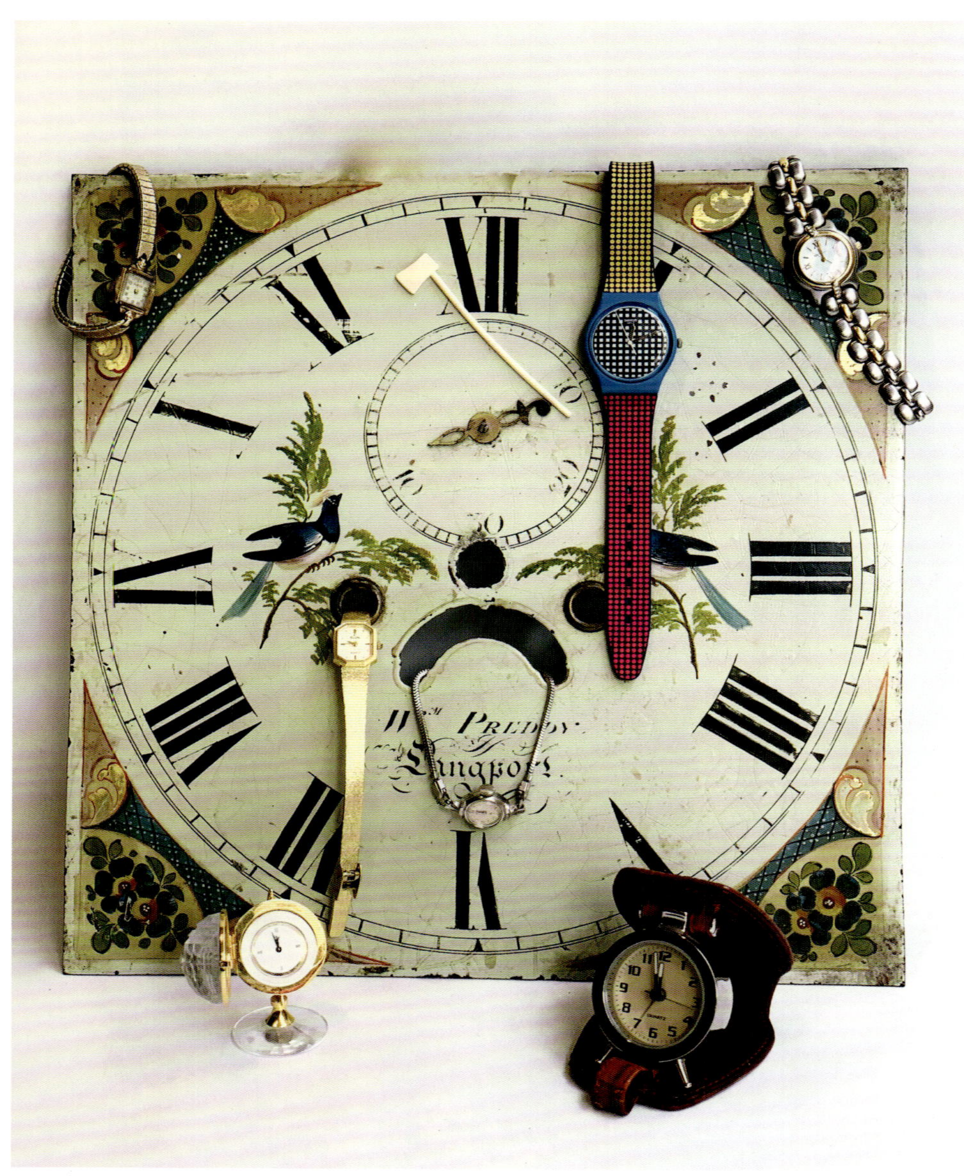

Time may be an illusion but it allows for good stories.

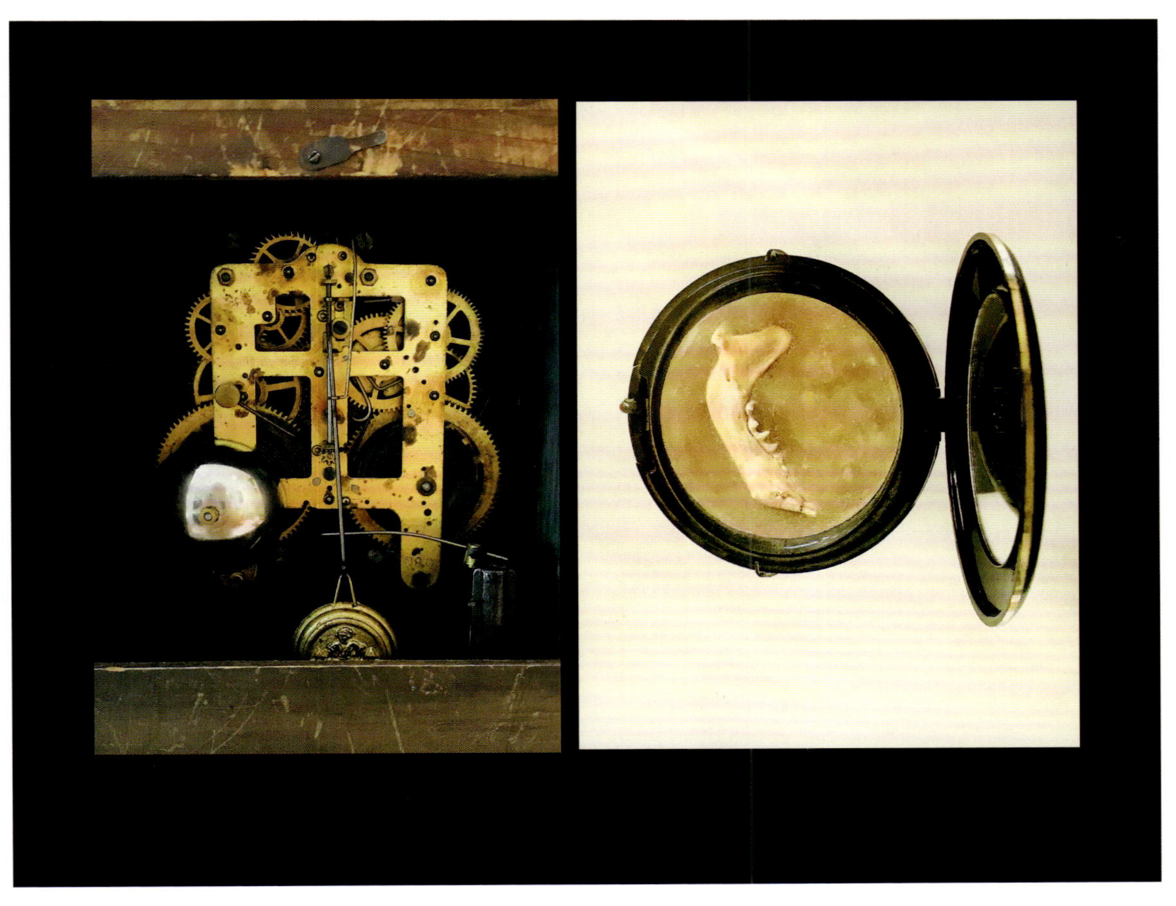

Time told by teeth.

—grandmother's wedding clock, Vanity *by Katherine Wimble Fox, 1999*

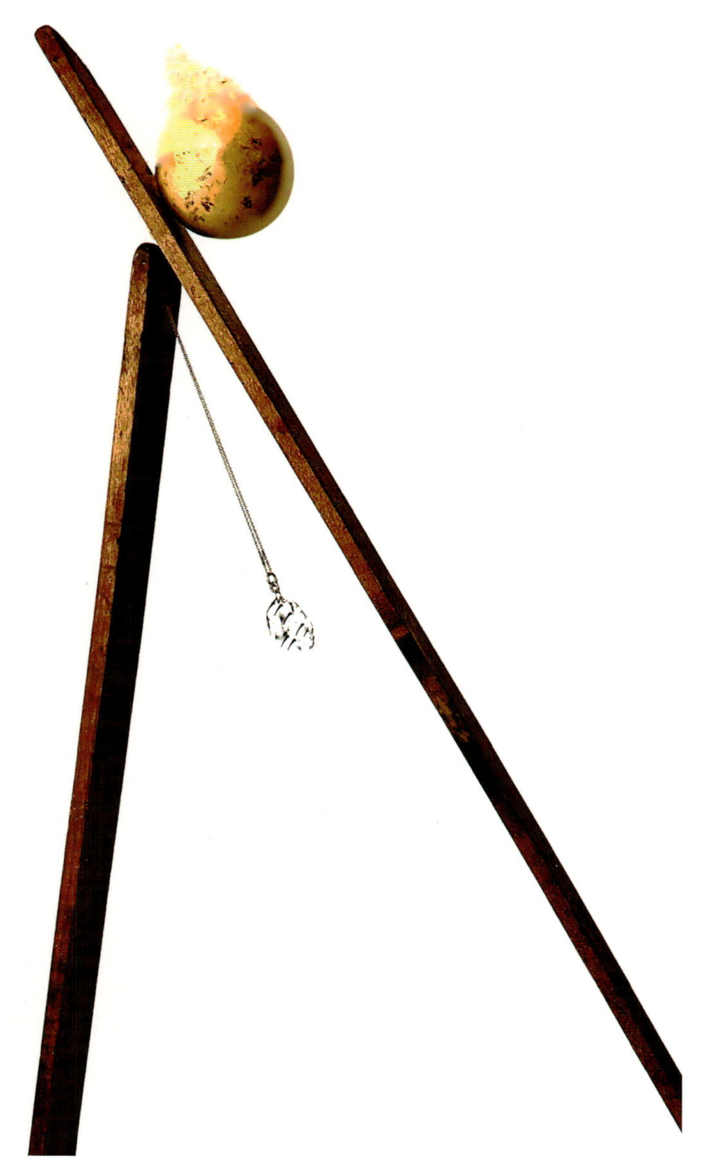

Our world is on fire. Up, down, over, roundabout, all uncertain.
We strive for balance like old measuring sticks supporting each other.

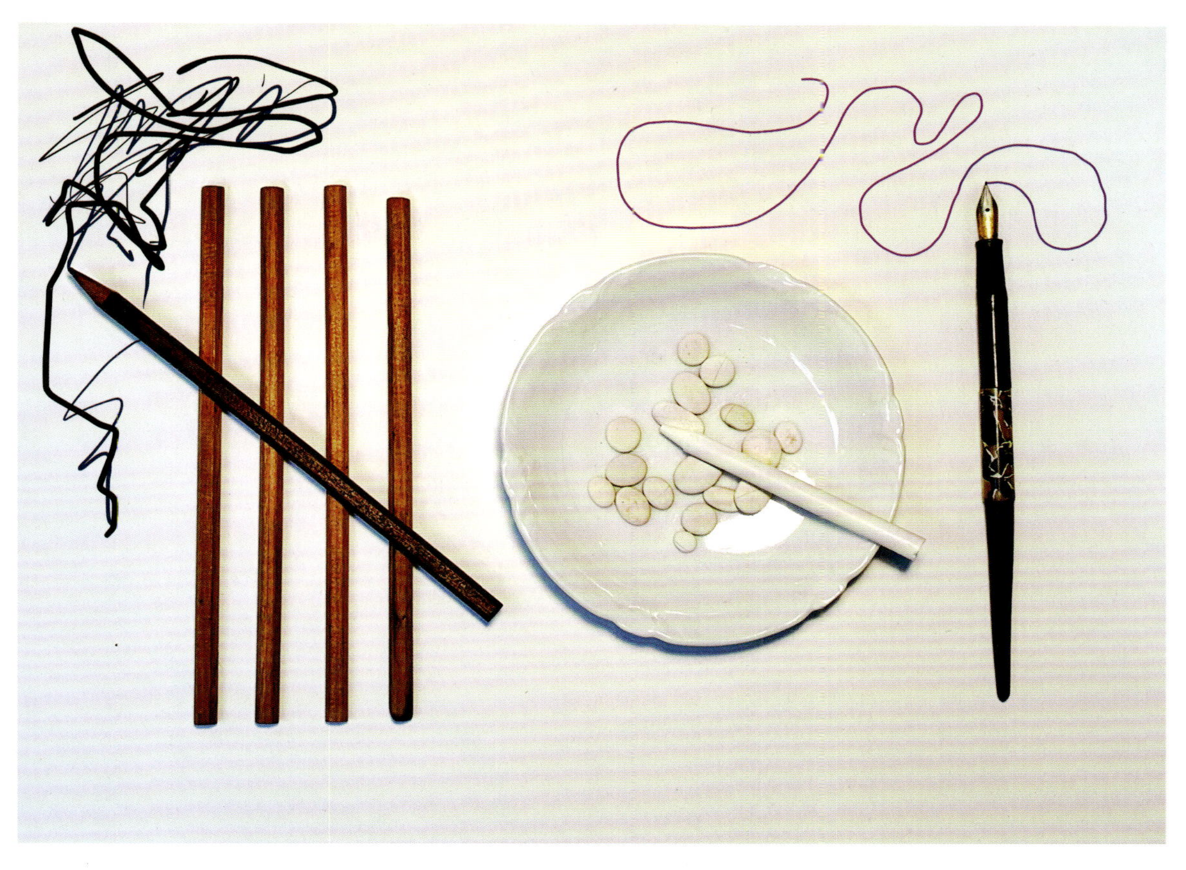

Are you a pen or pencil? Do you wiggle and squirm?
Can you be erased? How do you tell your story?

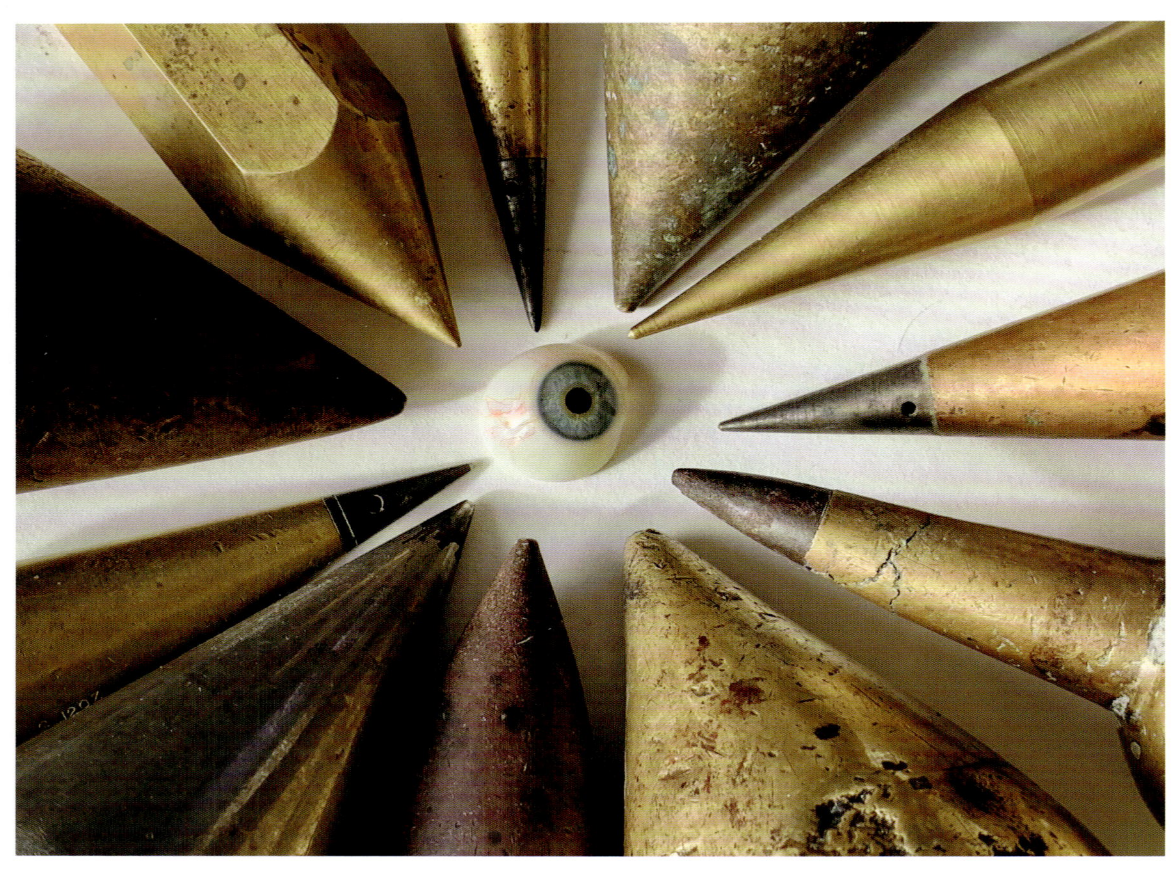

Save me! Tell me! Is my sin hubris or mediocrity?

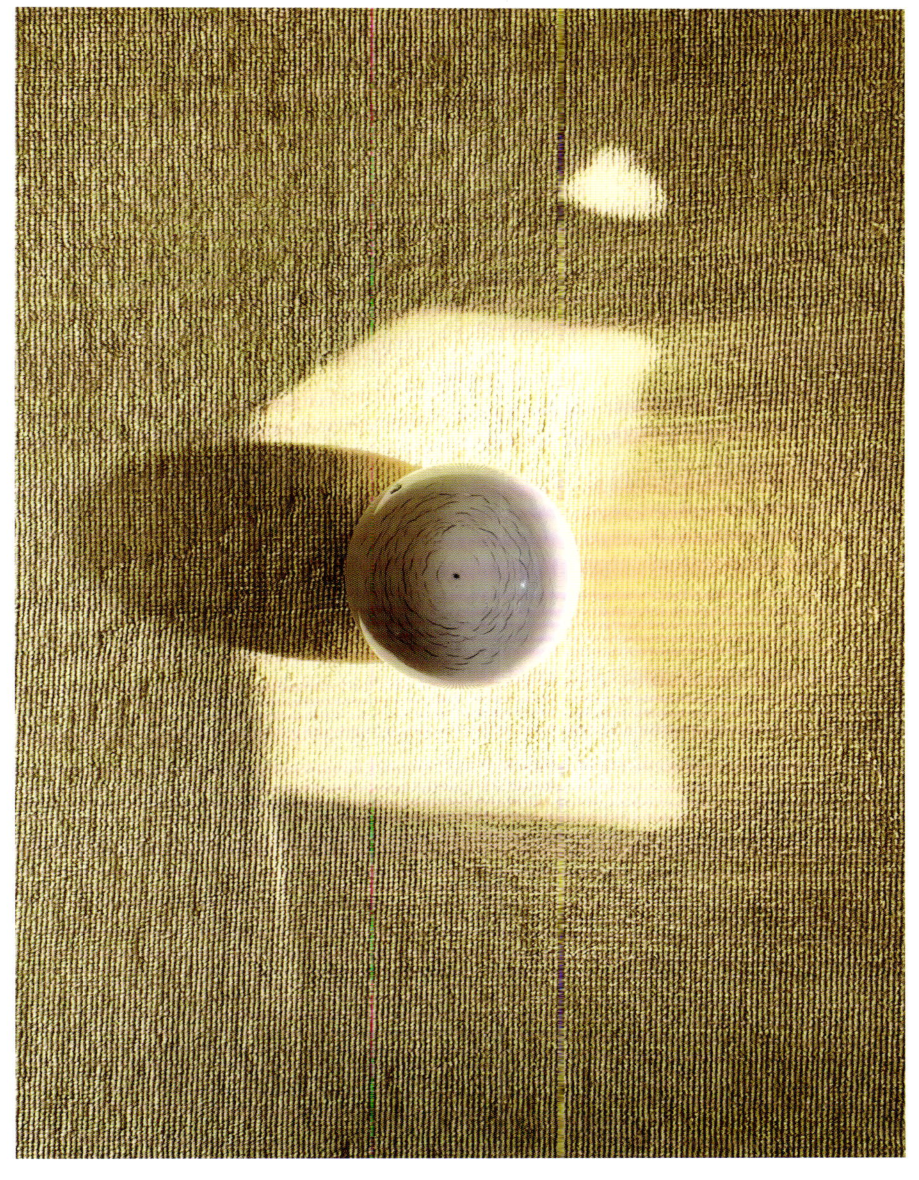

Beyond time and space has an infinitesimally small dot in which all time and space have ever resided. I don't know why it's there, but it is. Hardly significant at all.

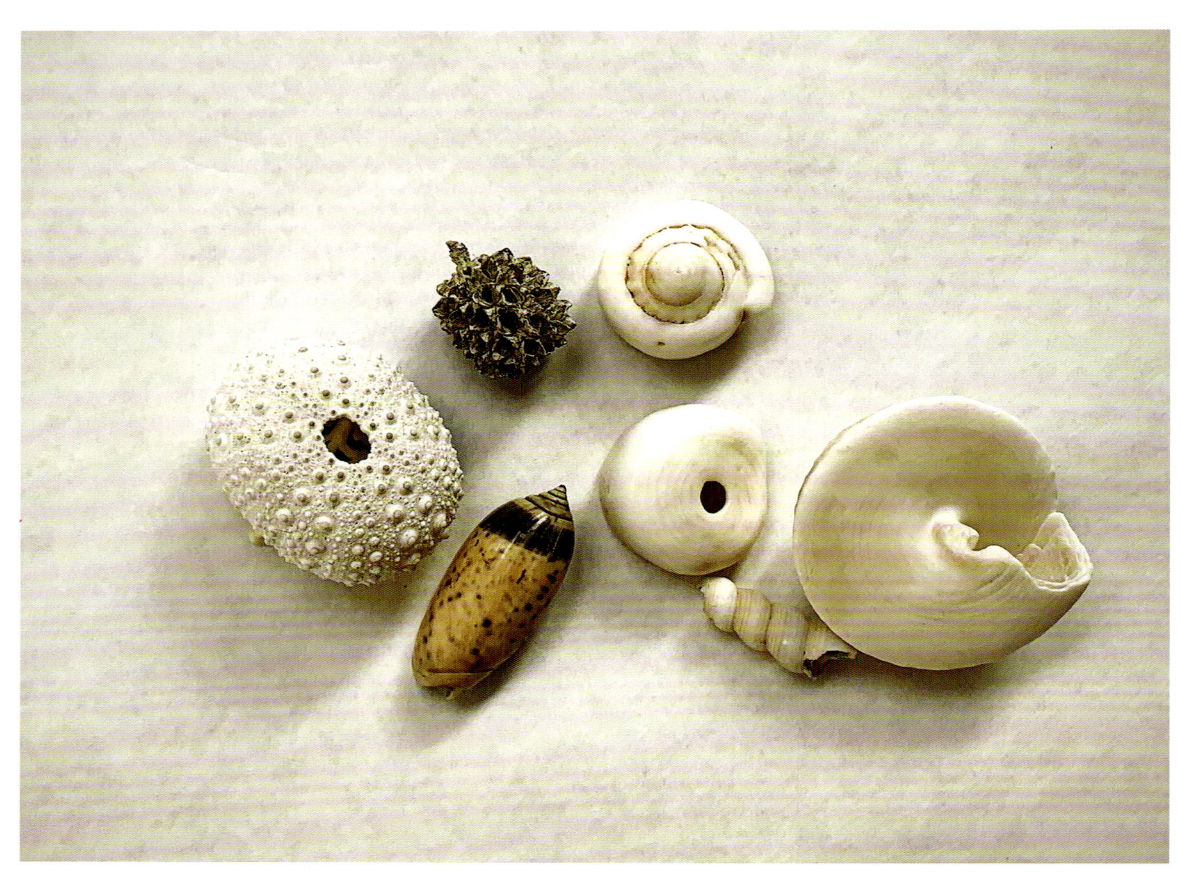

Nature is the proof of mathematics' elegance.

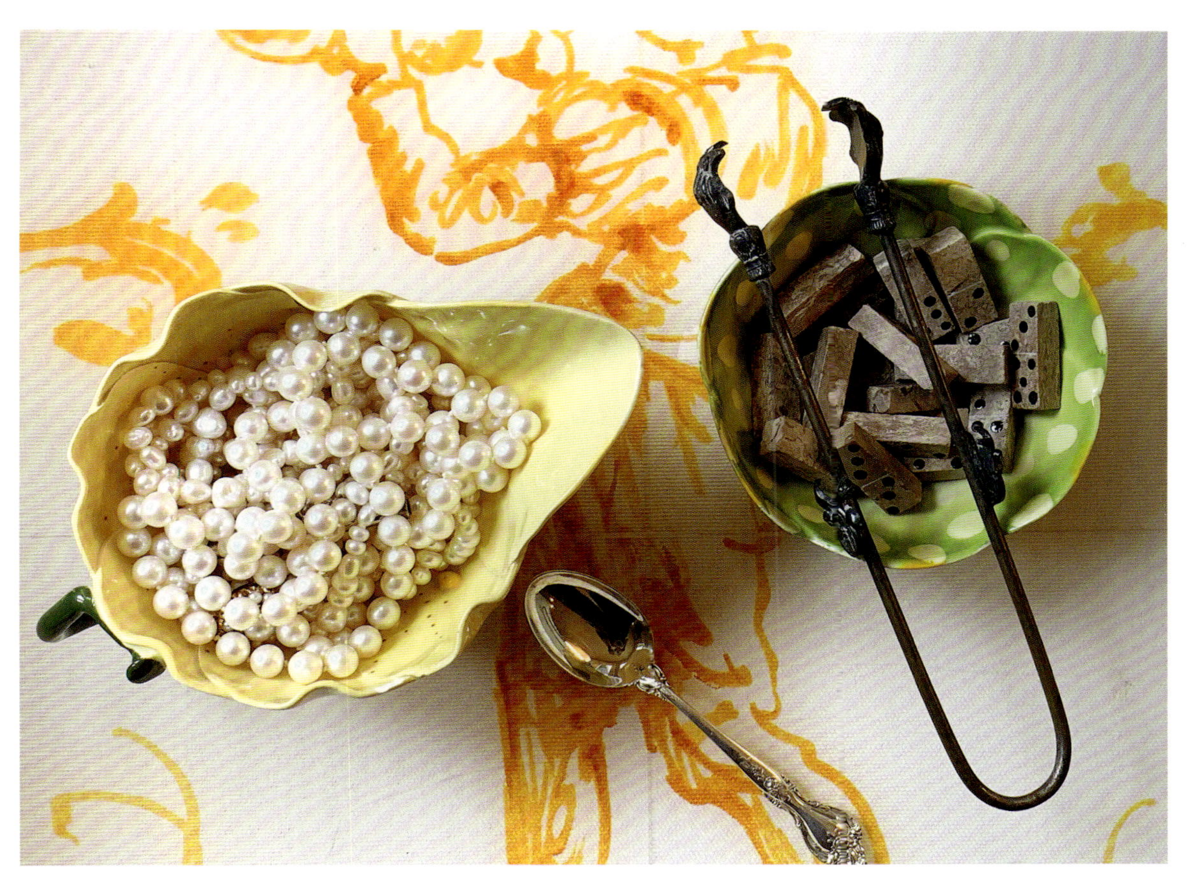

Luxury not shared is a prison.

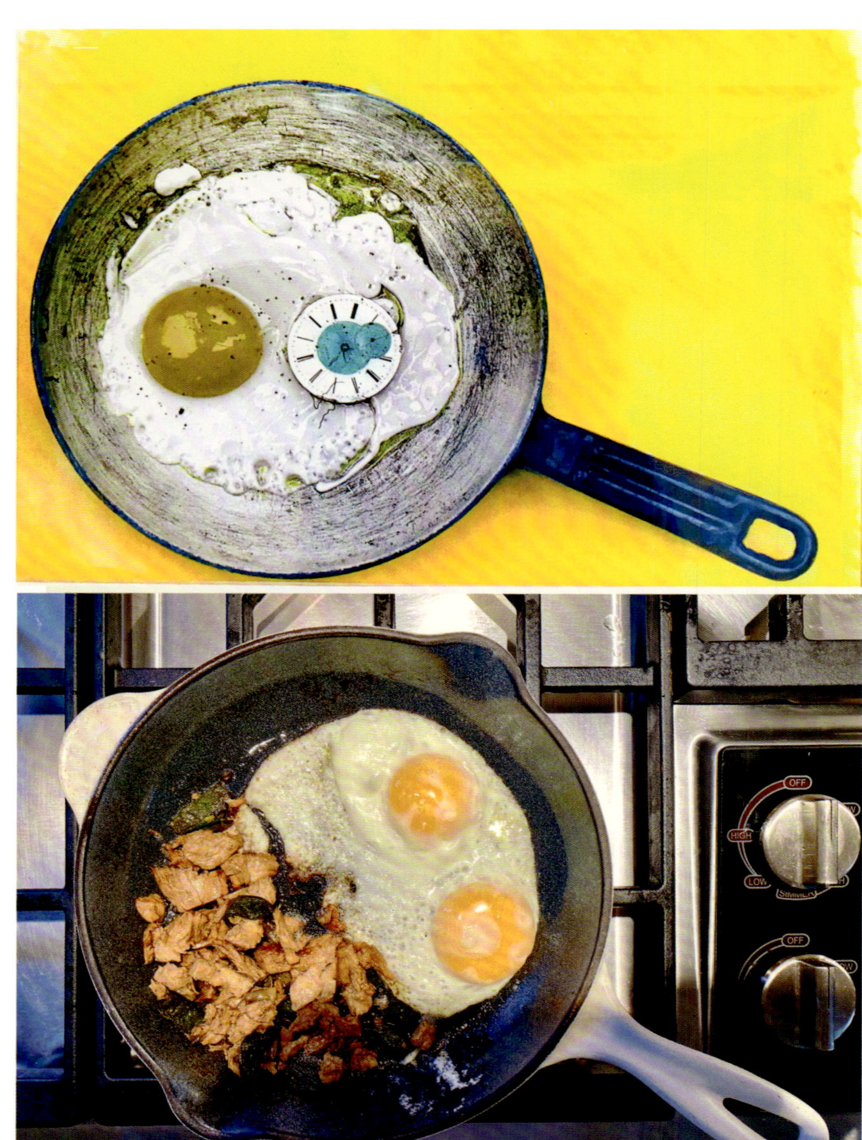

The egg came first.

—hand-colored photo, P. Z. Smith, 1973

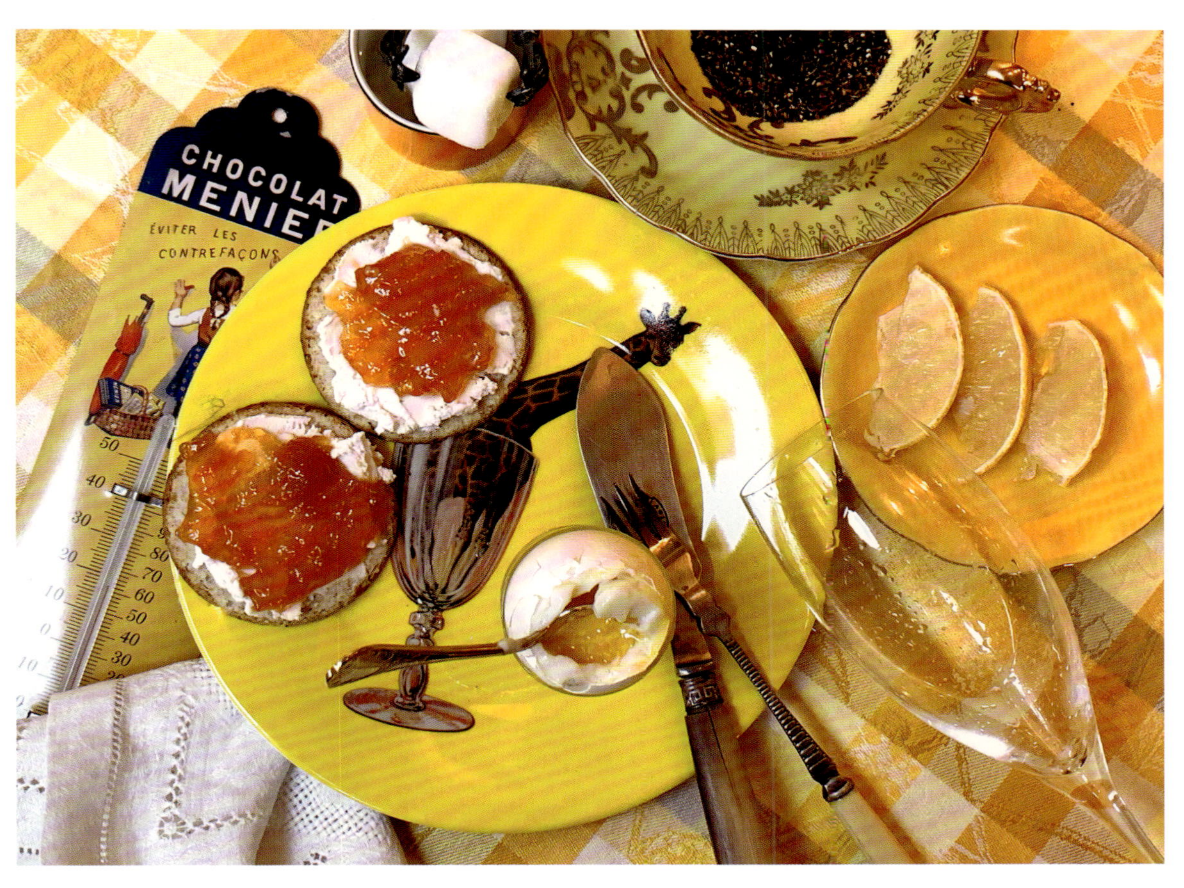

Brunch with Braque always started with champagne during his cubist period.

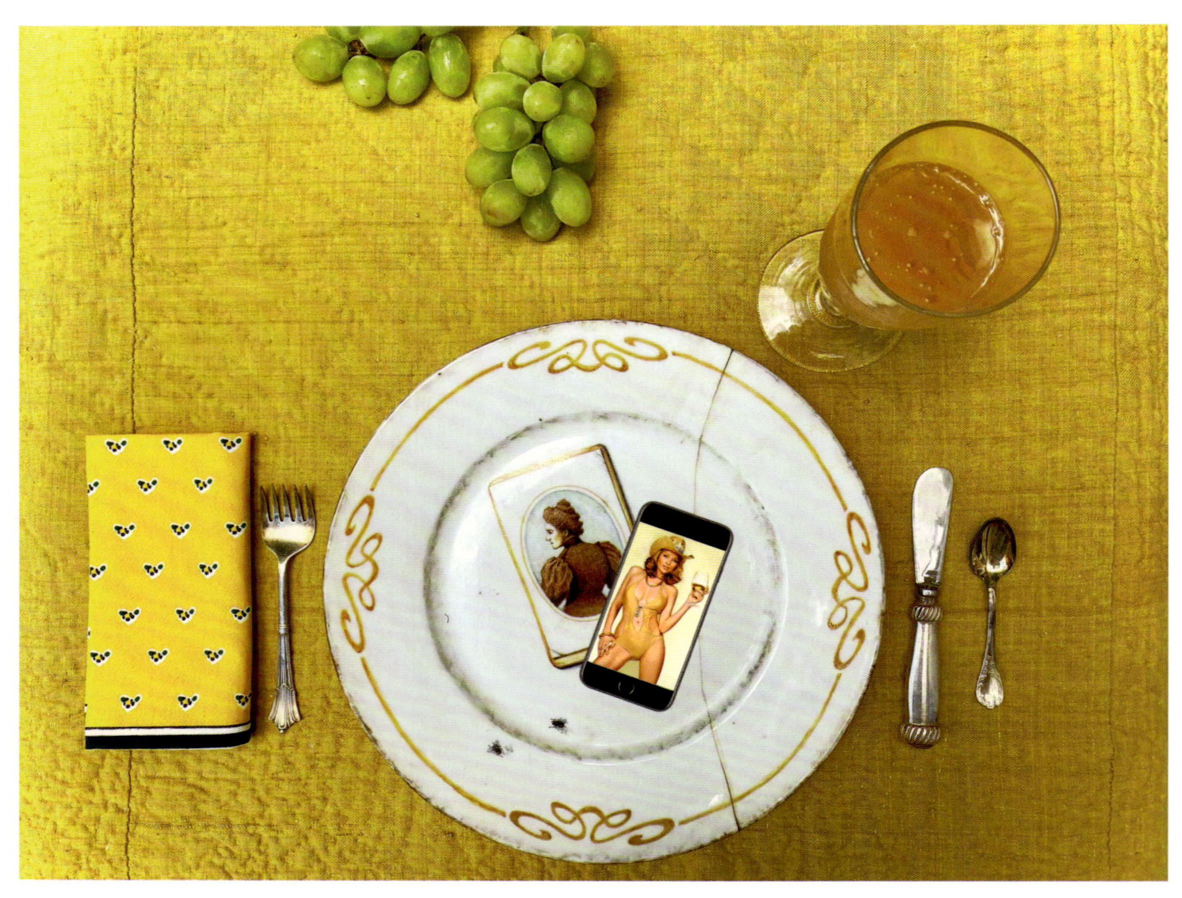

She loved to tease. She had done it through several lifetimes.

—hand-painted plate, Pierre Ducordeau, c. 2000

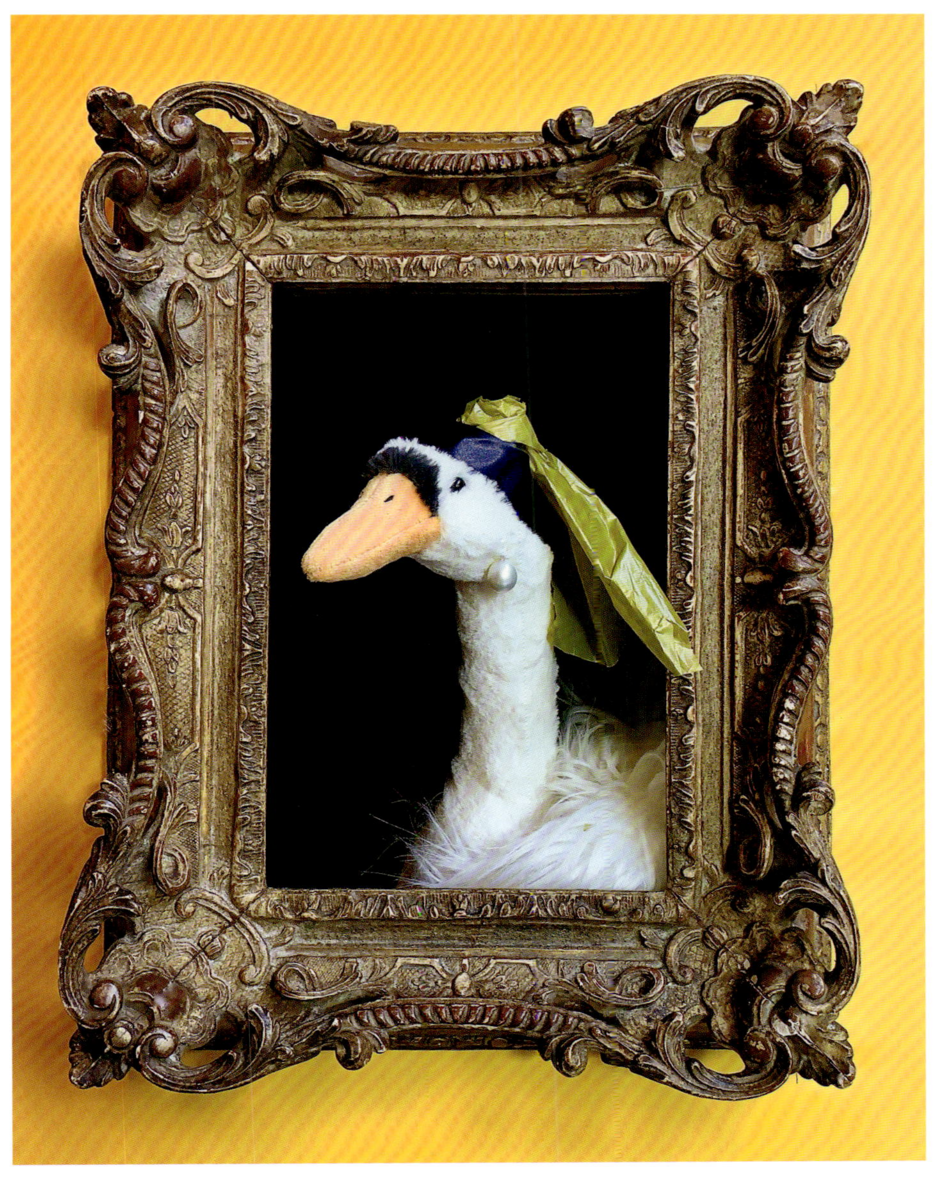

She was tired of being seen only for her beauty and, as a maid, preferred to discover what beauty she had in the privacy of her chambers. She gave the barnyard gander, hopelessly in love, her earring and asked him to stand in for her. People see what they expect to see.

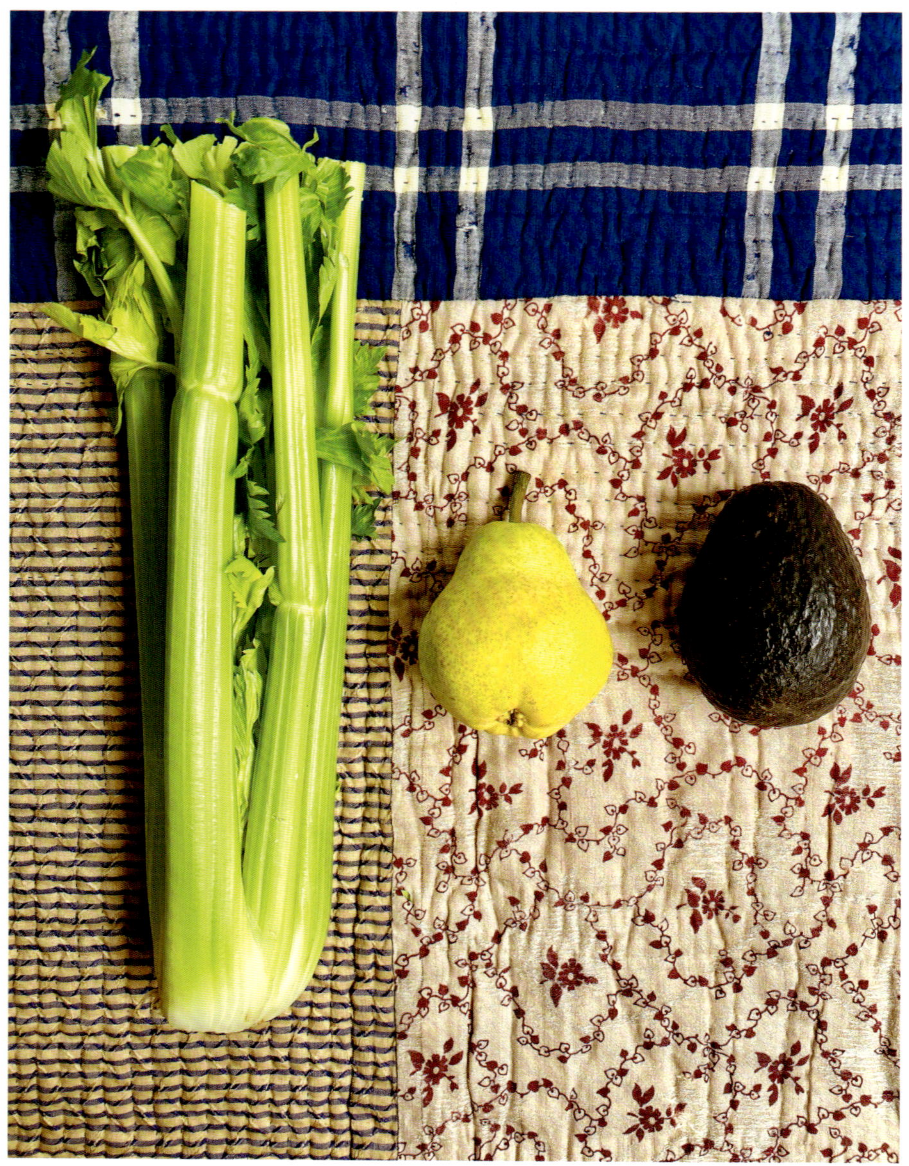

The basics are the basics—cooking, cleaning, having babies, burying people, attempting poetry when sorrow is not enough.

—on silk and wool, French, c.1820

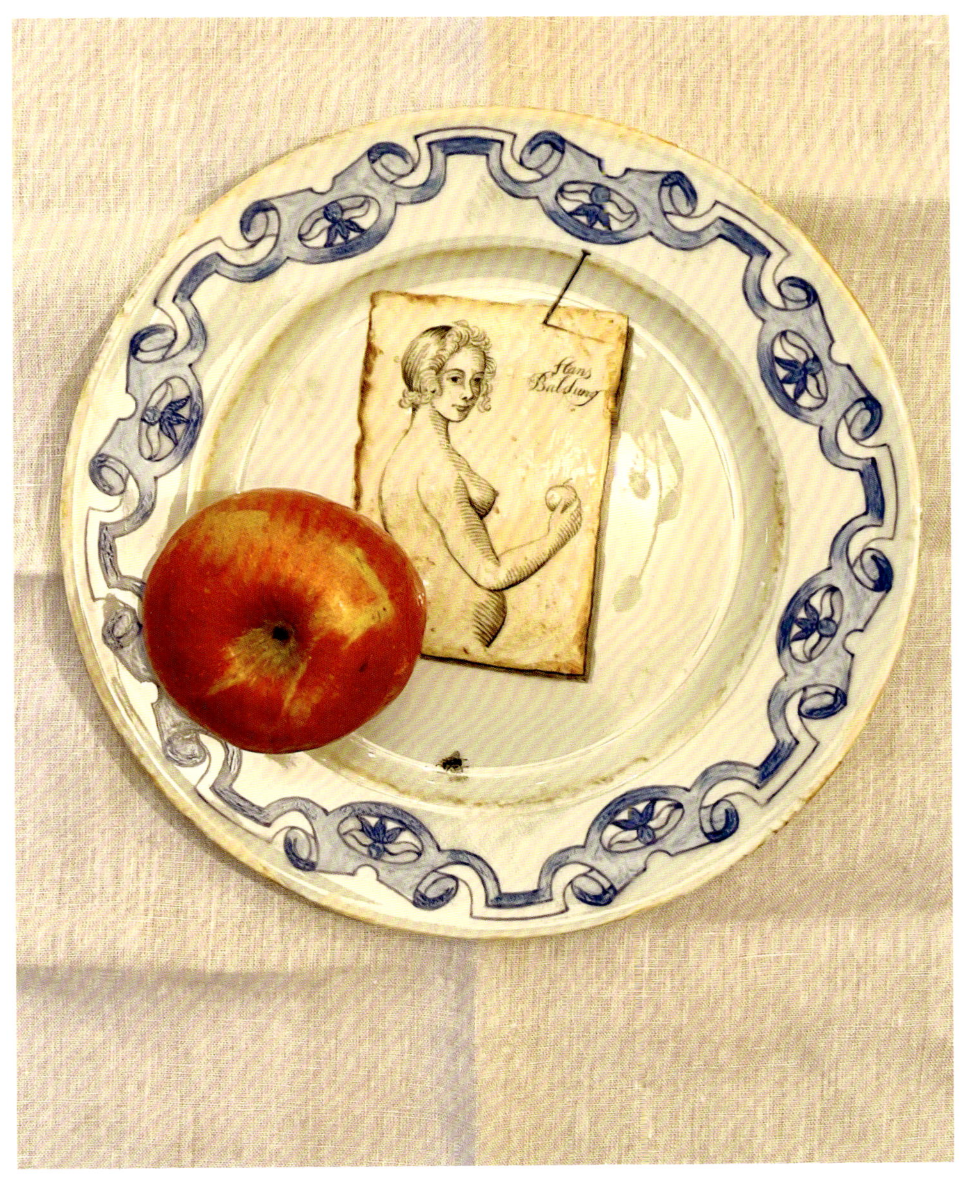

The apple, rich in vitamin C, and boron for bone growth,
has been tainted by accusations of seduction from the beginning,
as though the female libido requires an apple when a pear or peach would do.

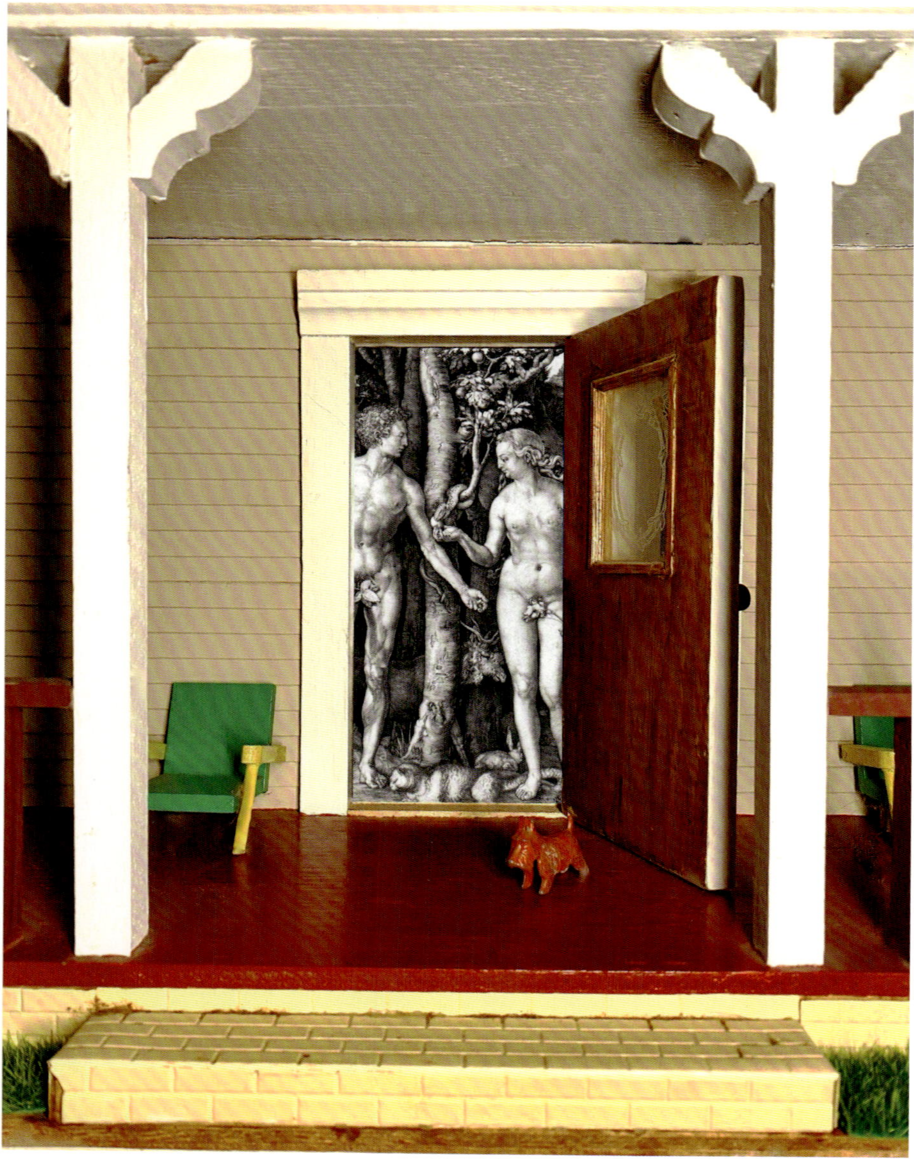

After they ate the fruit of self-awareness and knew themselves—and each other—they moved to a bungalow where they became recluses, sure no one would believe their story.

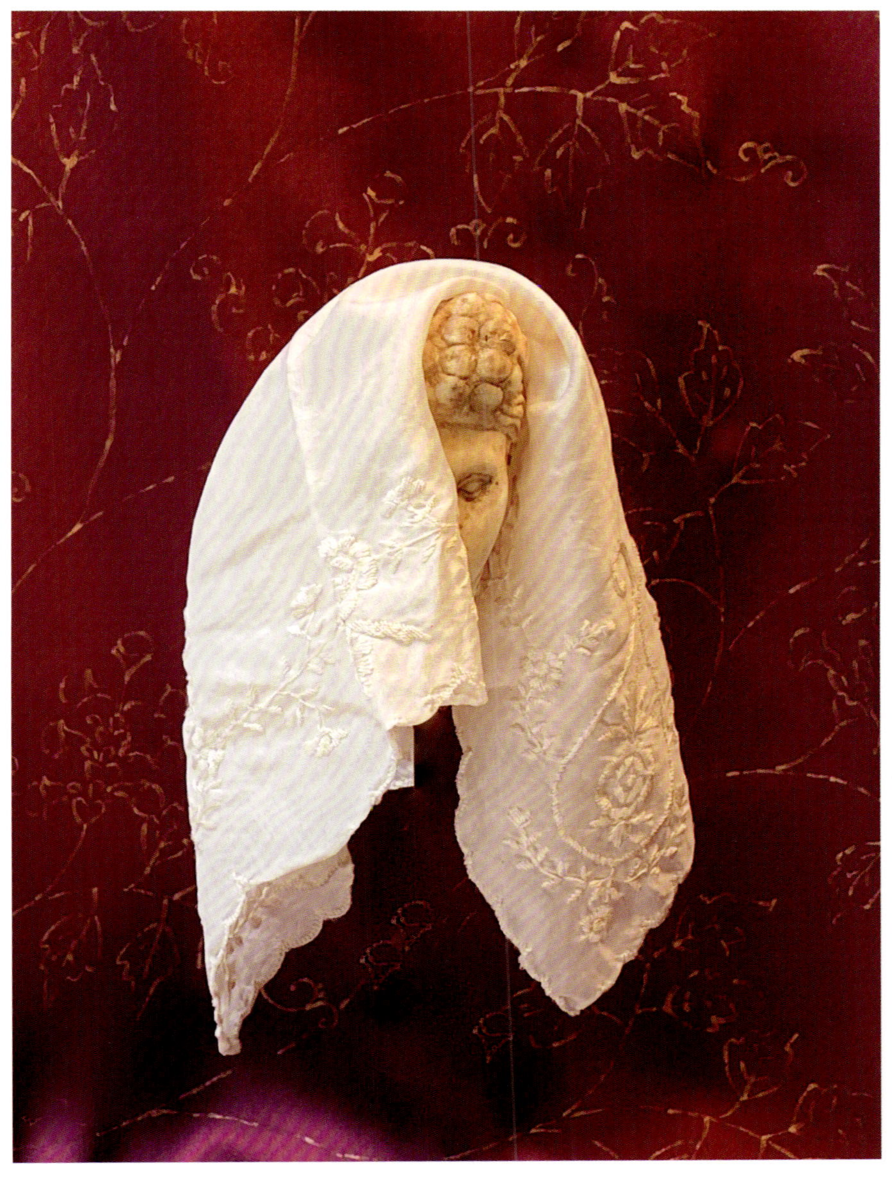

They told her it was safe, but who were they to force her into cultures of finance, disease, people killing people? They had never shown they knew anything about her.

—ivory bust, Roman

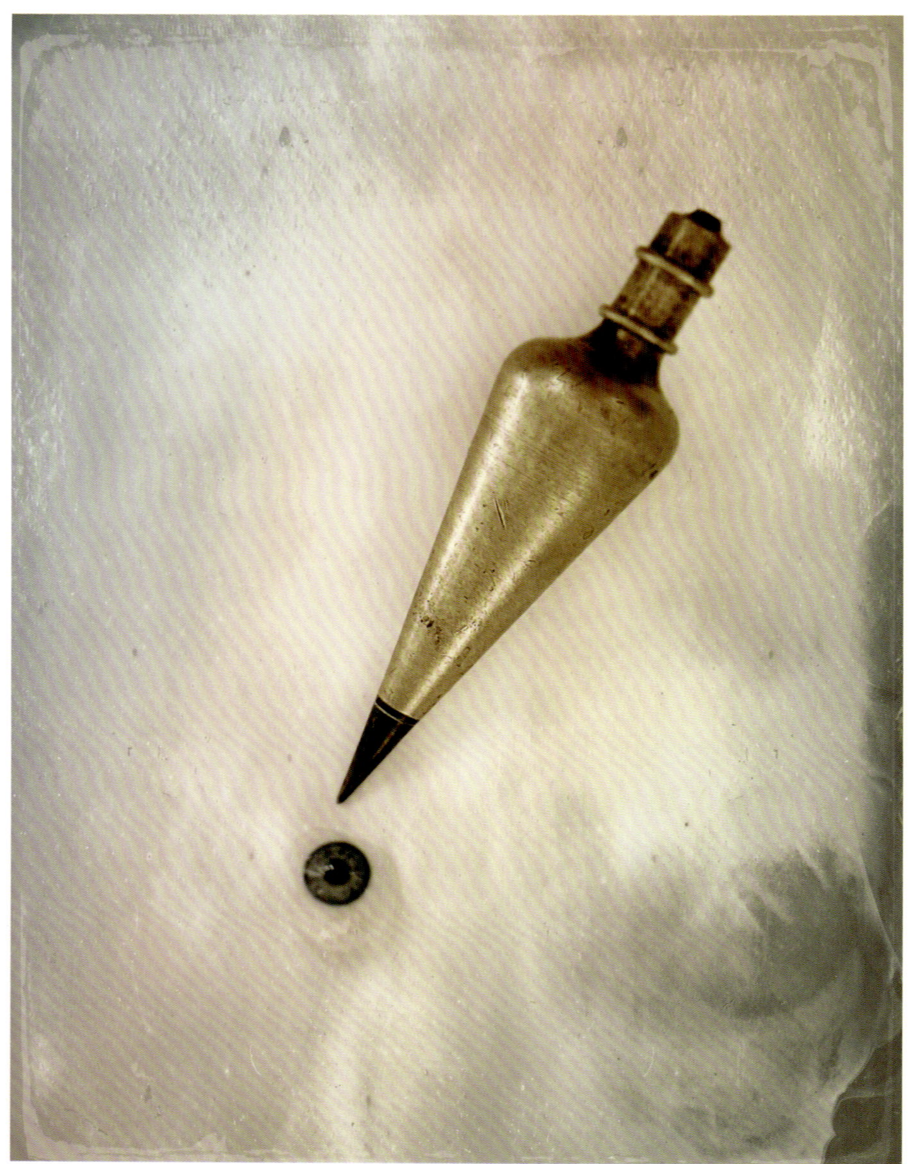

When Mystery turns its gaze on you, you will be shot through.
In that instant you will see terrifying grandeur as It claims you.

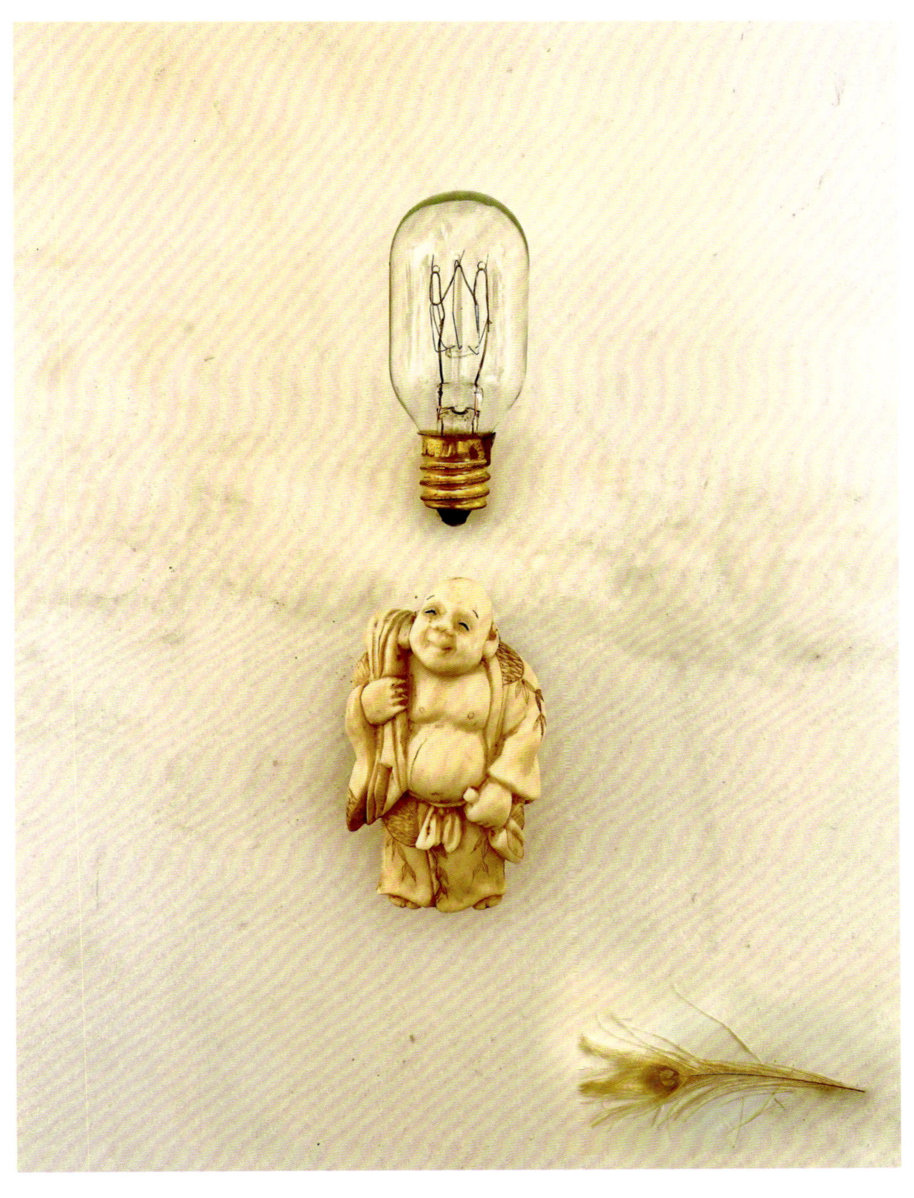

Let the idea be the idea and the feather be the feather. Buddha smiled.

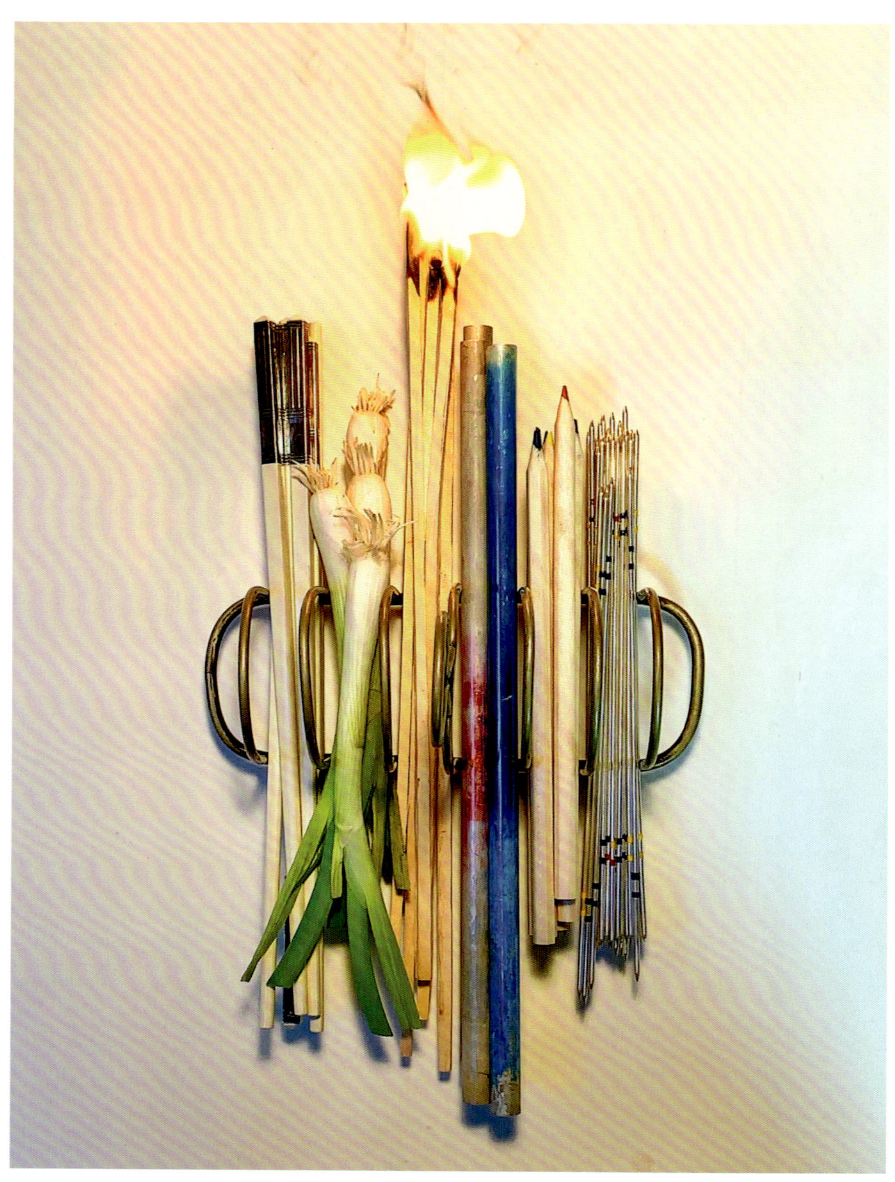

Linear objects have commonalities, beginnings and ends, directions. They are functional.

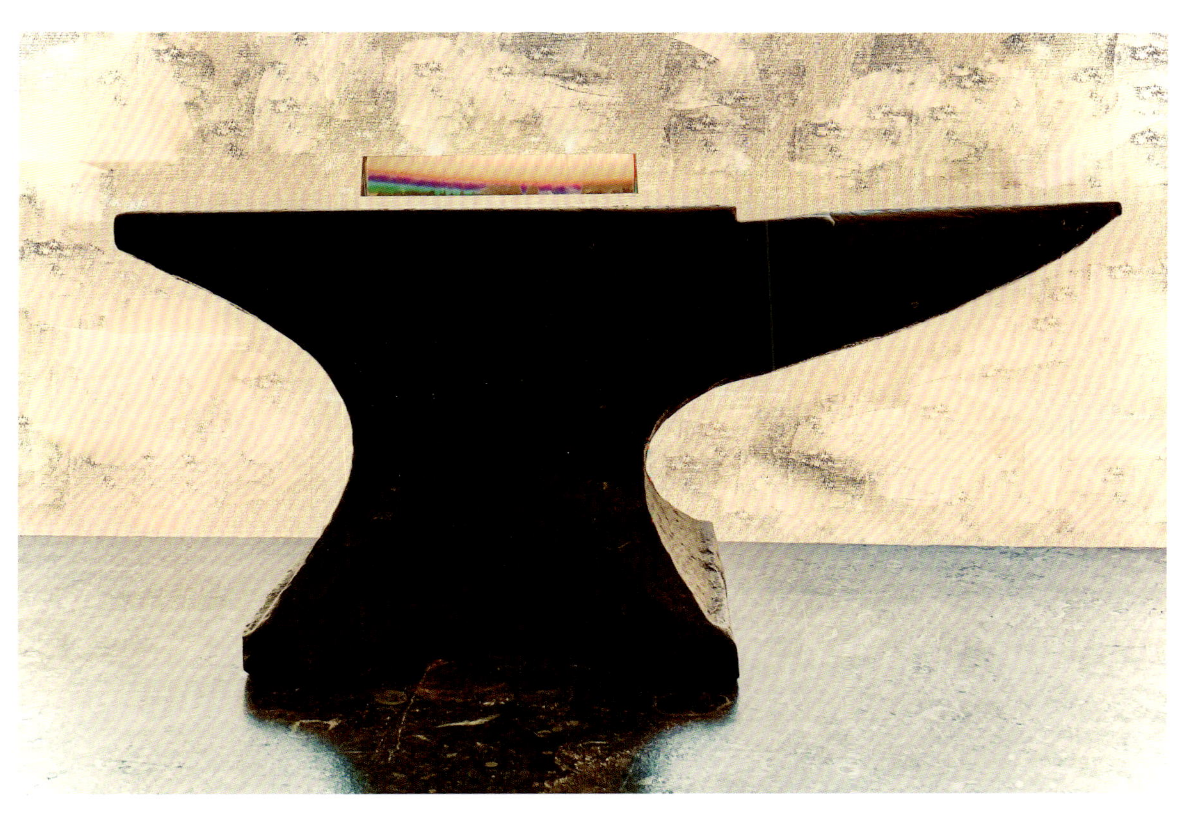

An anvil too heavy to lift, crowned by a prism of light.

—through four generations of sons until claimed by a daughter

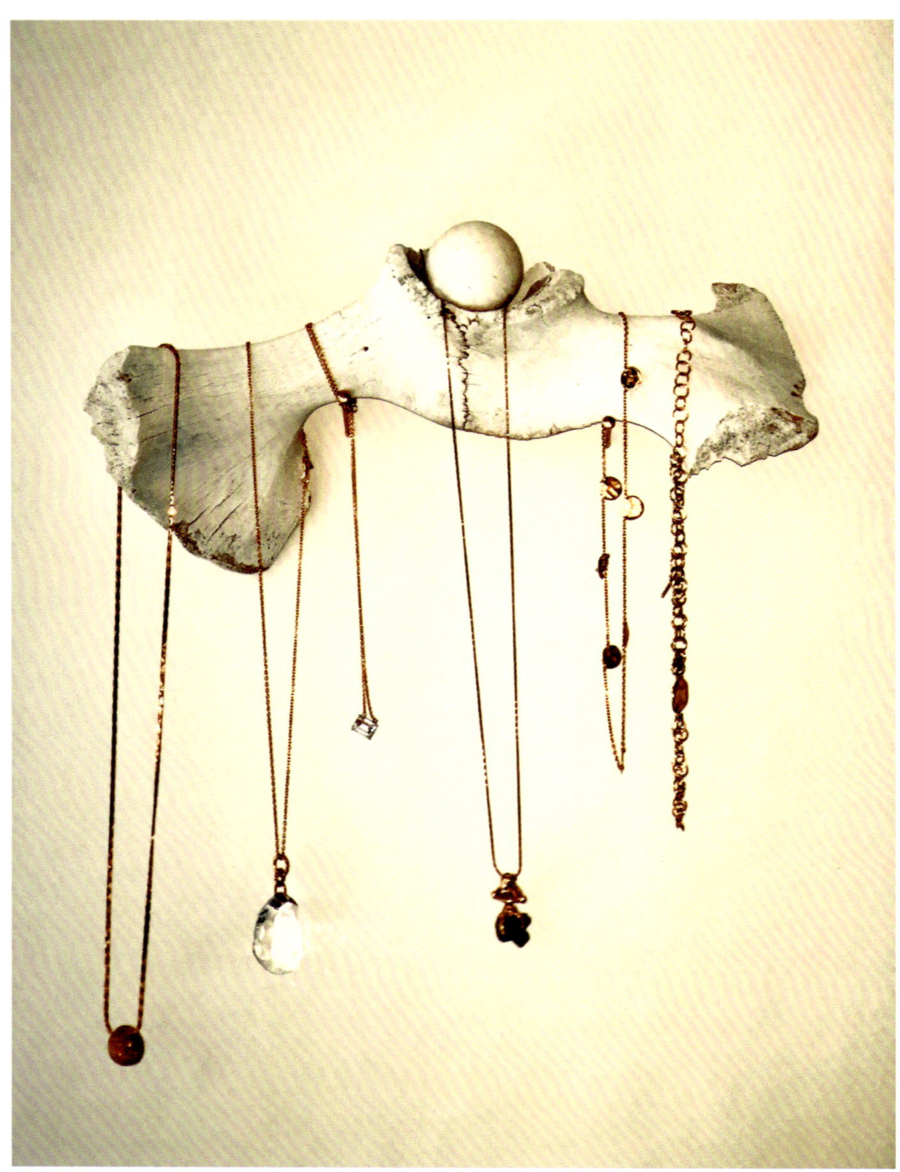

We swing on the bones of the past.

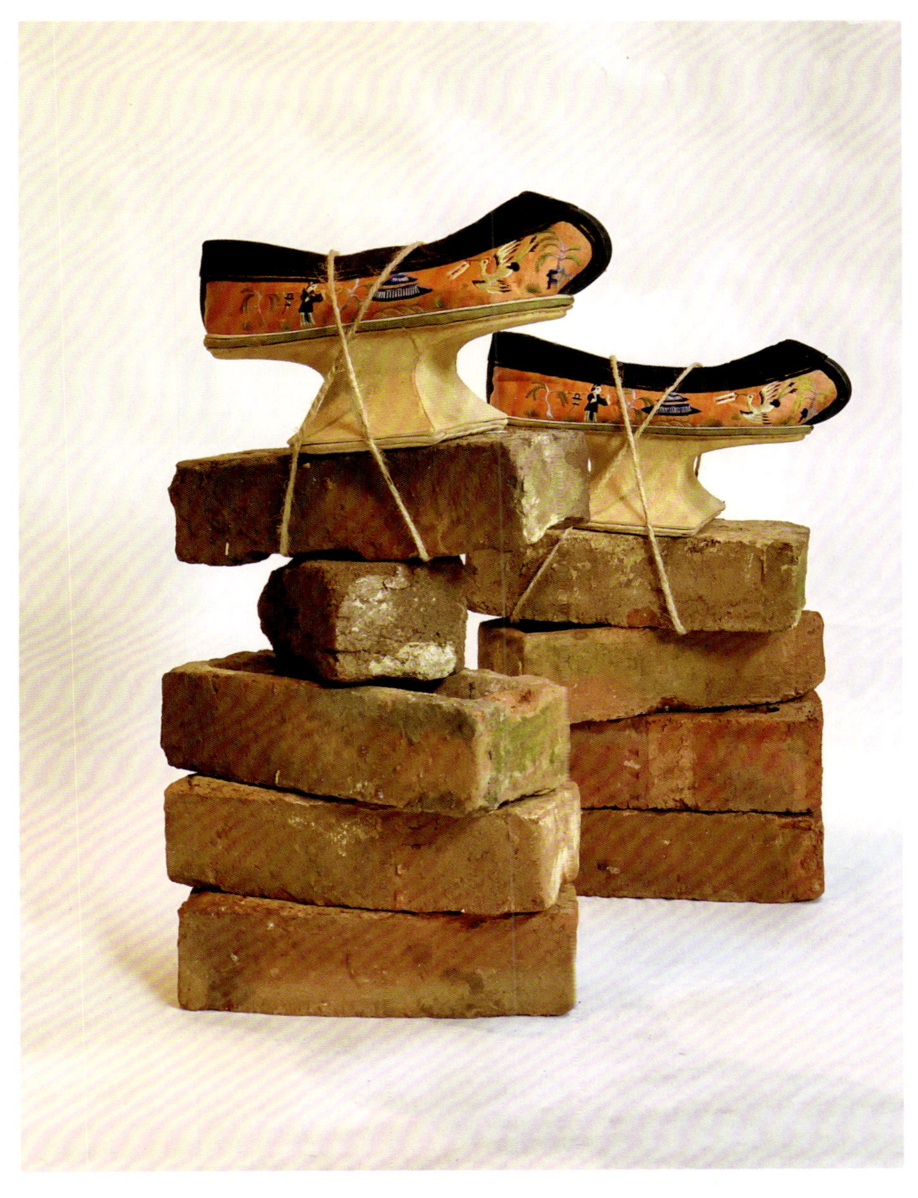

Their feet were molded by crushing their bones and souls.
When the girls screamed, their mouths were bound too.

—10th century to mid-20th century China

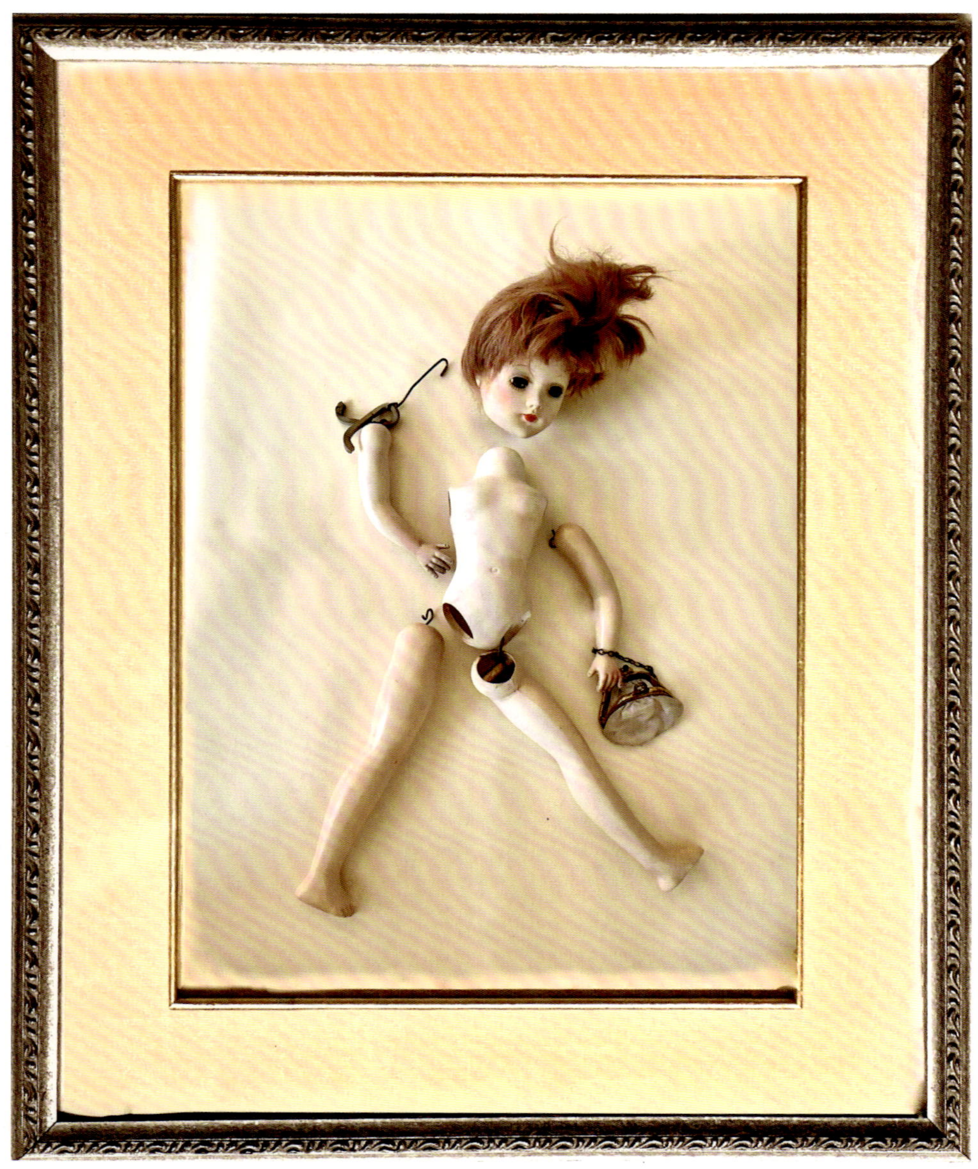

She entered vengeance like Gretel, leaving pieces of herself behind to be picked up when she found her way back.

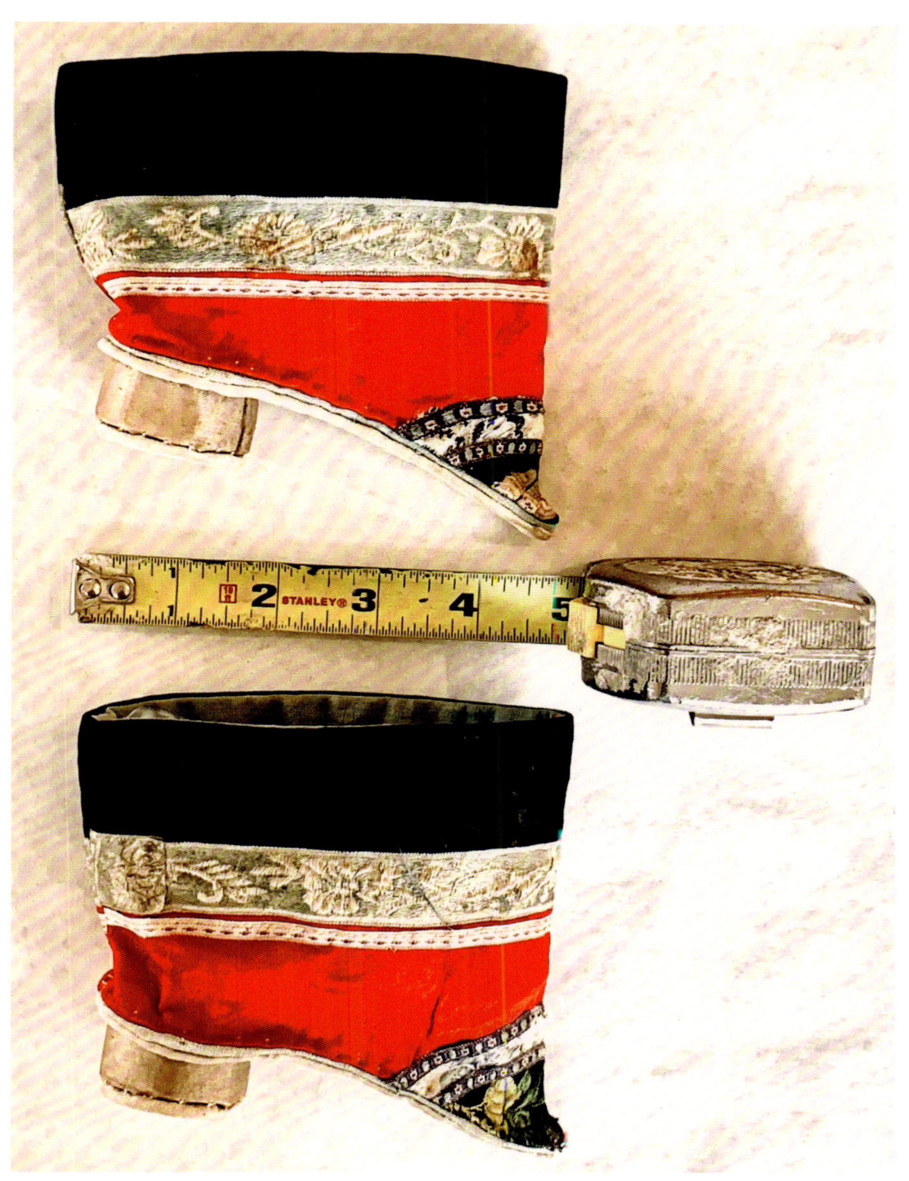

Outrage!

Dislocated objects bring their cultures with them, like refugees.

—mother's tea cup, moose antler

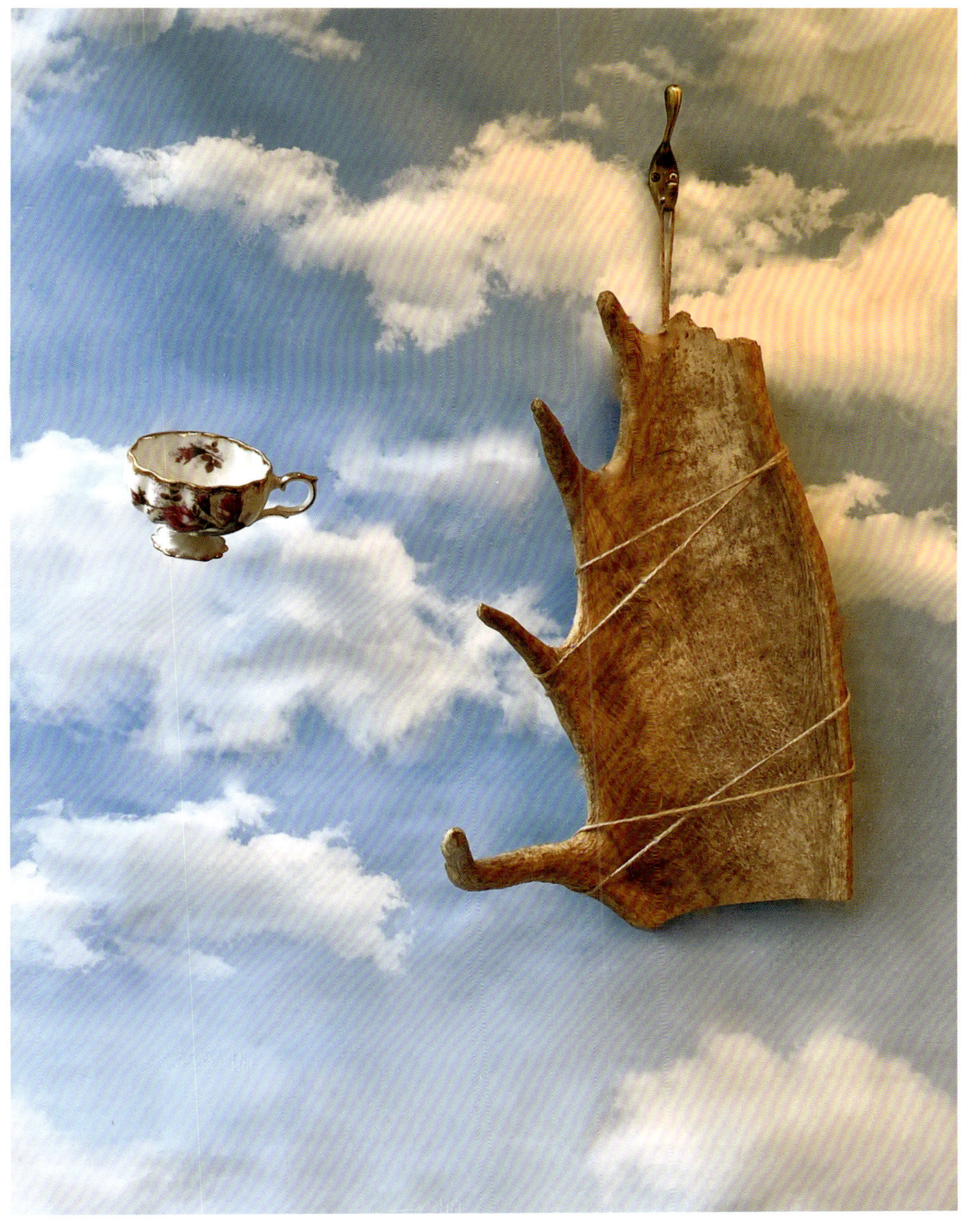

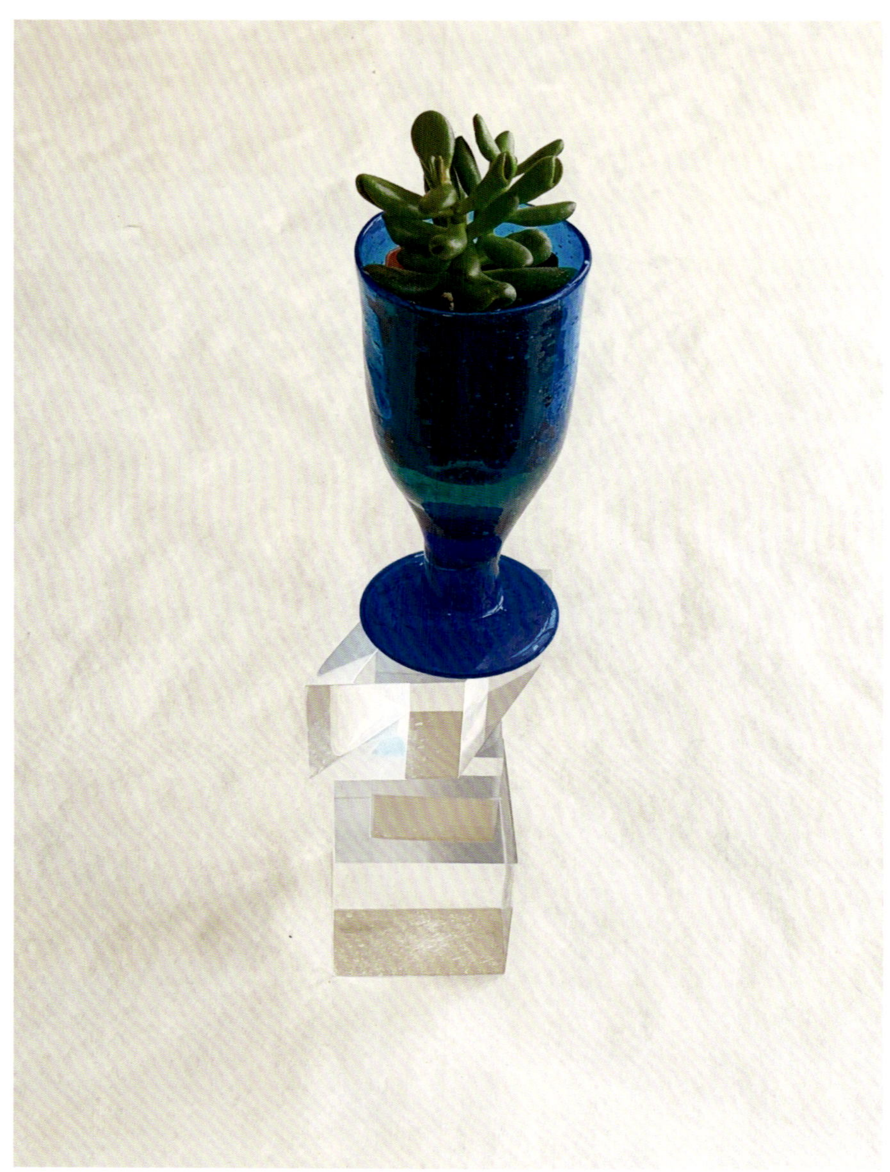

She asked so little, expected less—but when no one was watching, she rose to unimaginable heights.

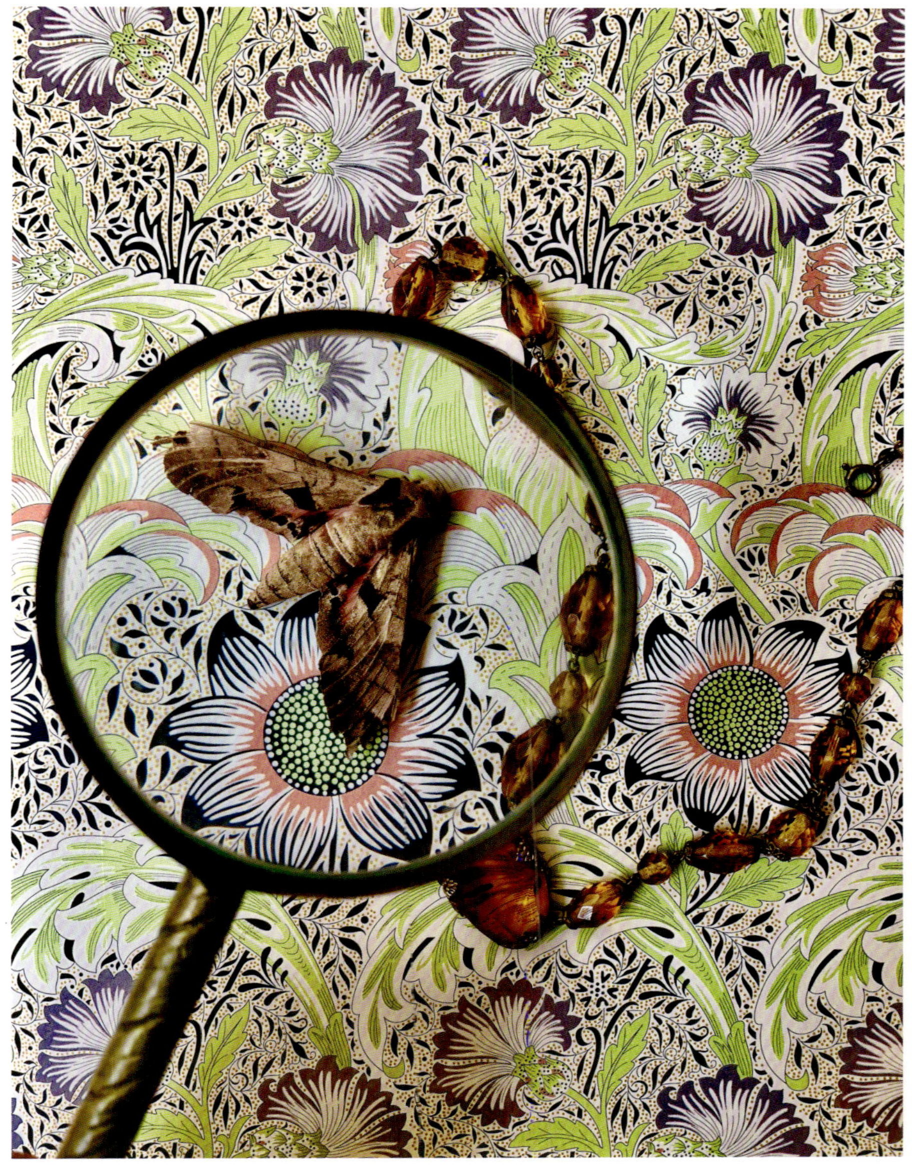

The sphinx moth reveled so deliciously in the new fabric he never realized he was the most closely observed.

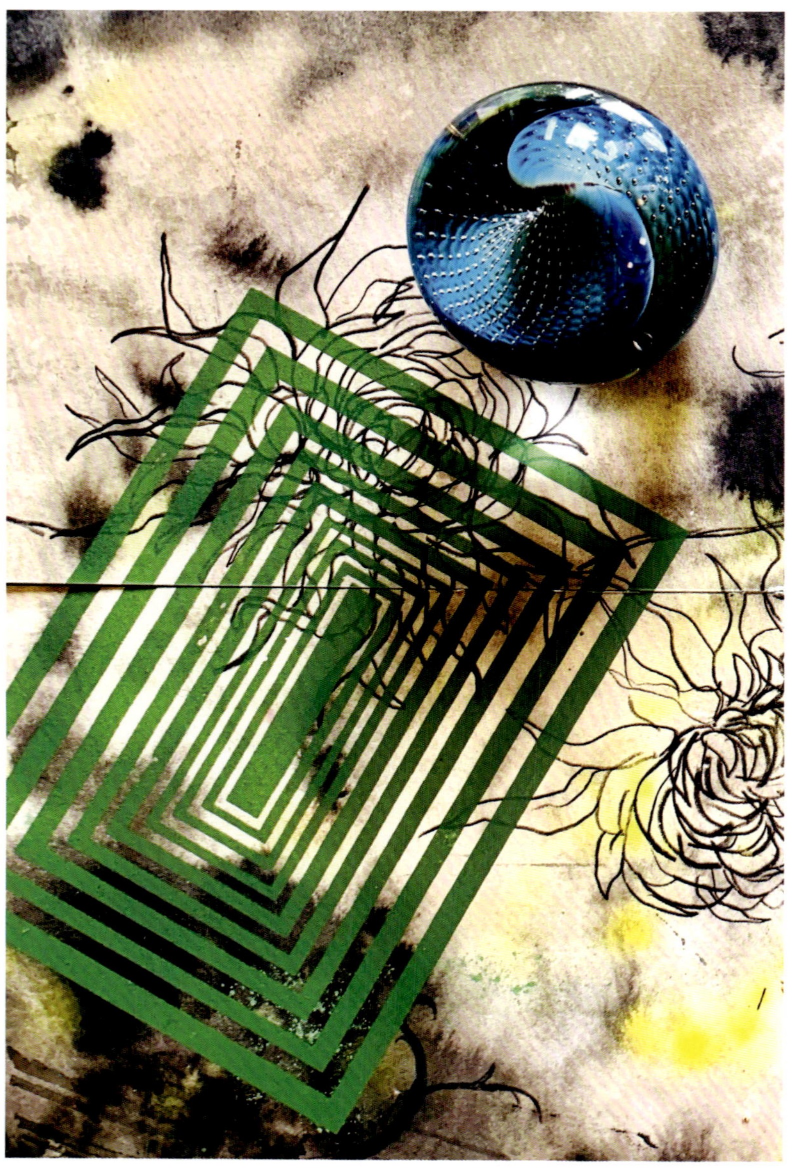

Yin and yang in a glass globe.

—watercolor by Julie Wolfe, 2018

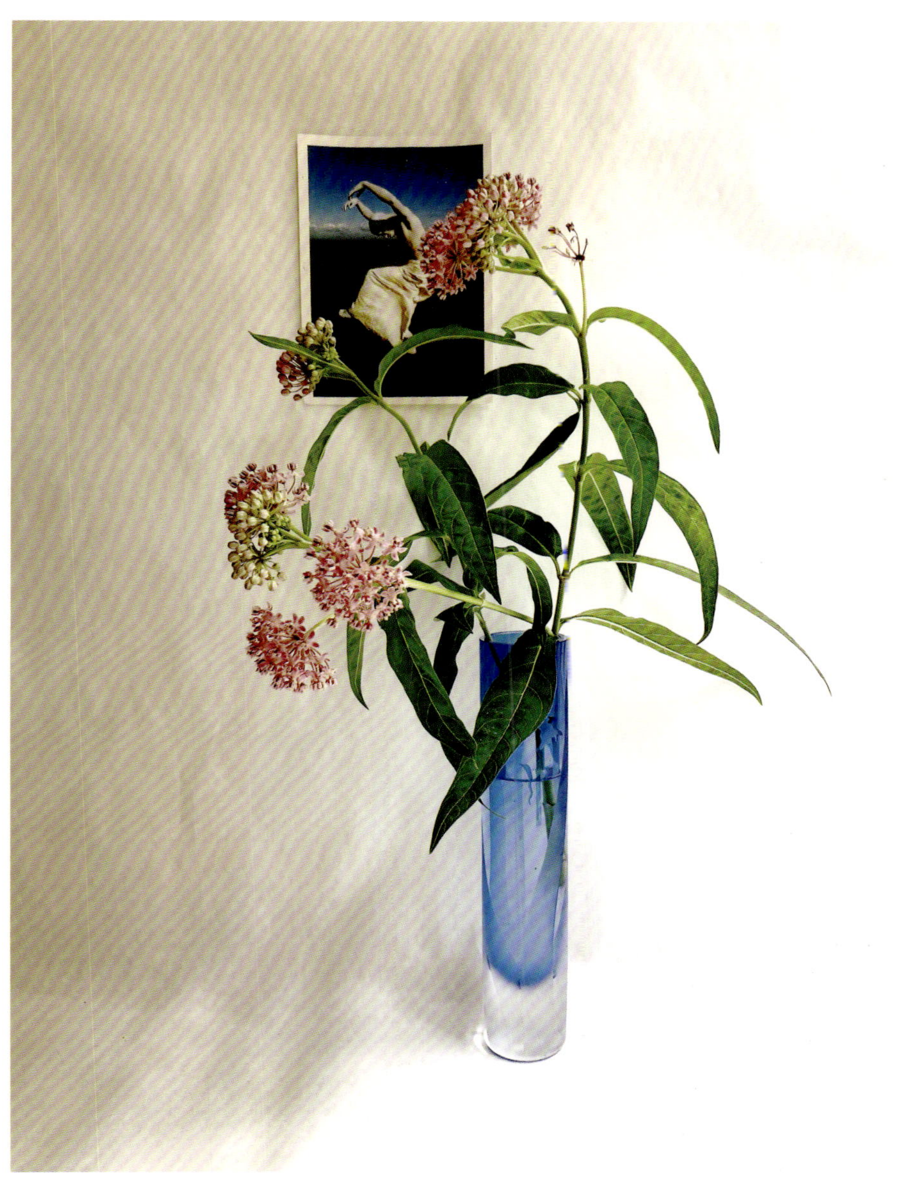

Bend like a willow. . .or a swamp milkweed.

—Sankai Juku, Butoh Troupe dancer

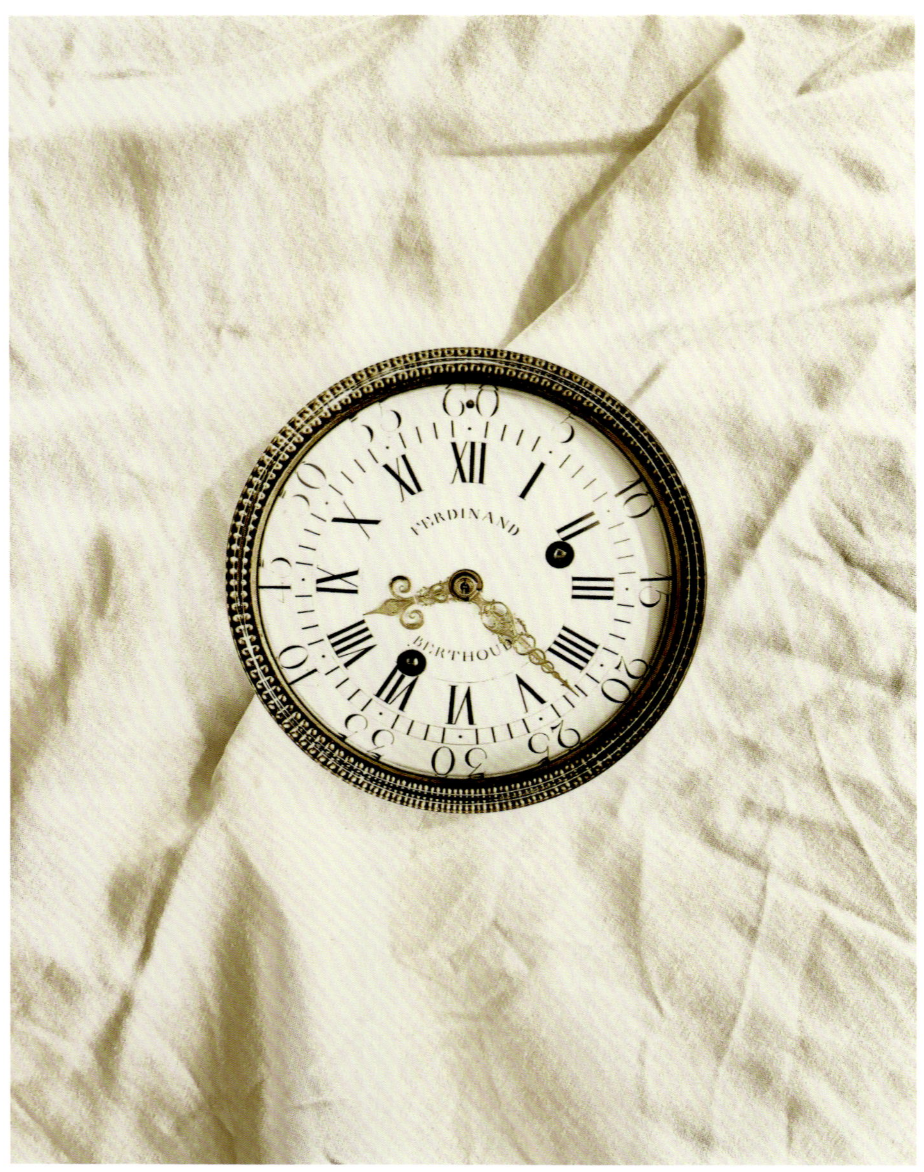

Time wrinkles our linen with its every breath.

—A Wrinkle in Time, *Ursula le Guin*

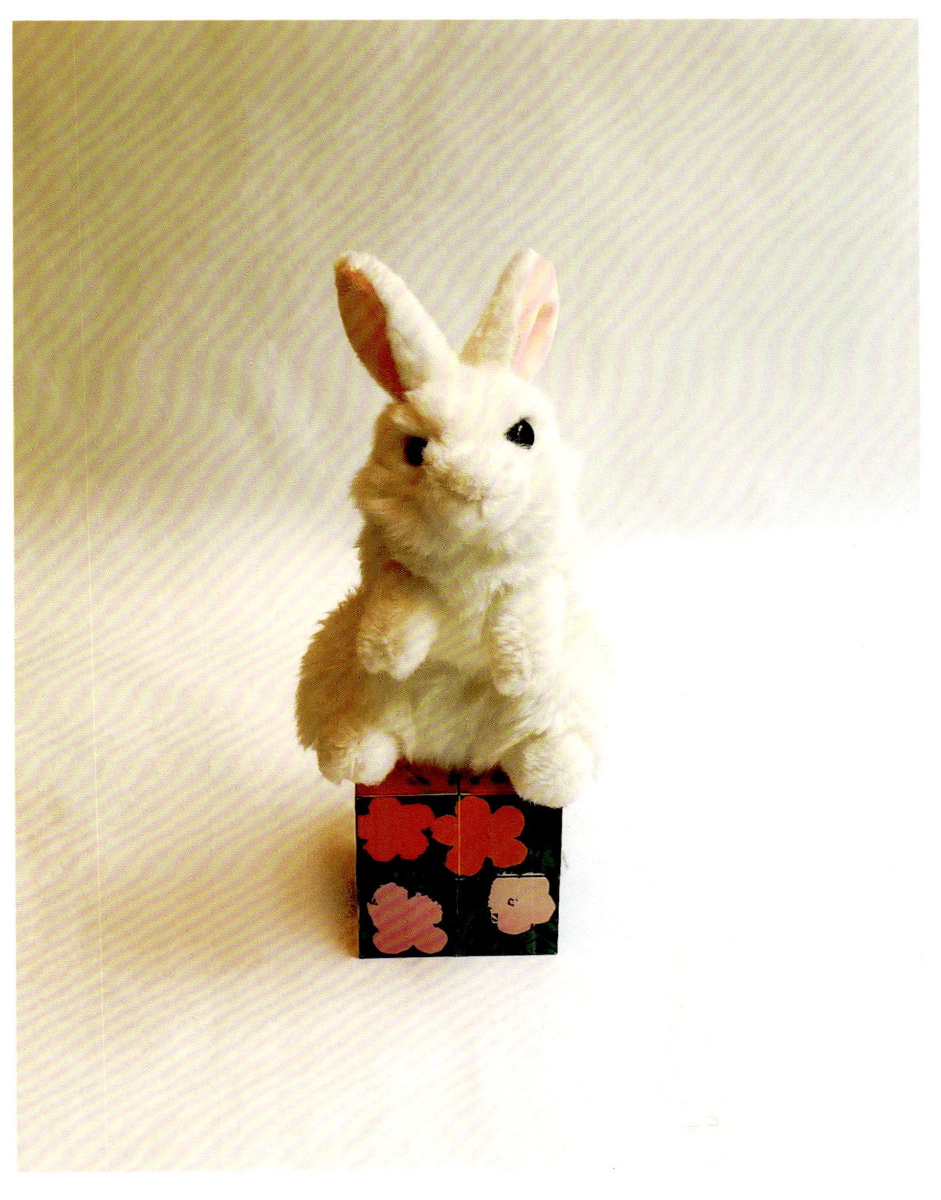

Late again! It's driving me mad! I'll miss the lemon crumpets!

—*musing on* Alice

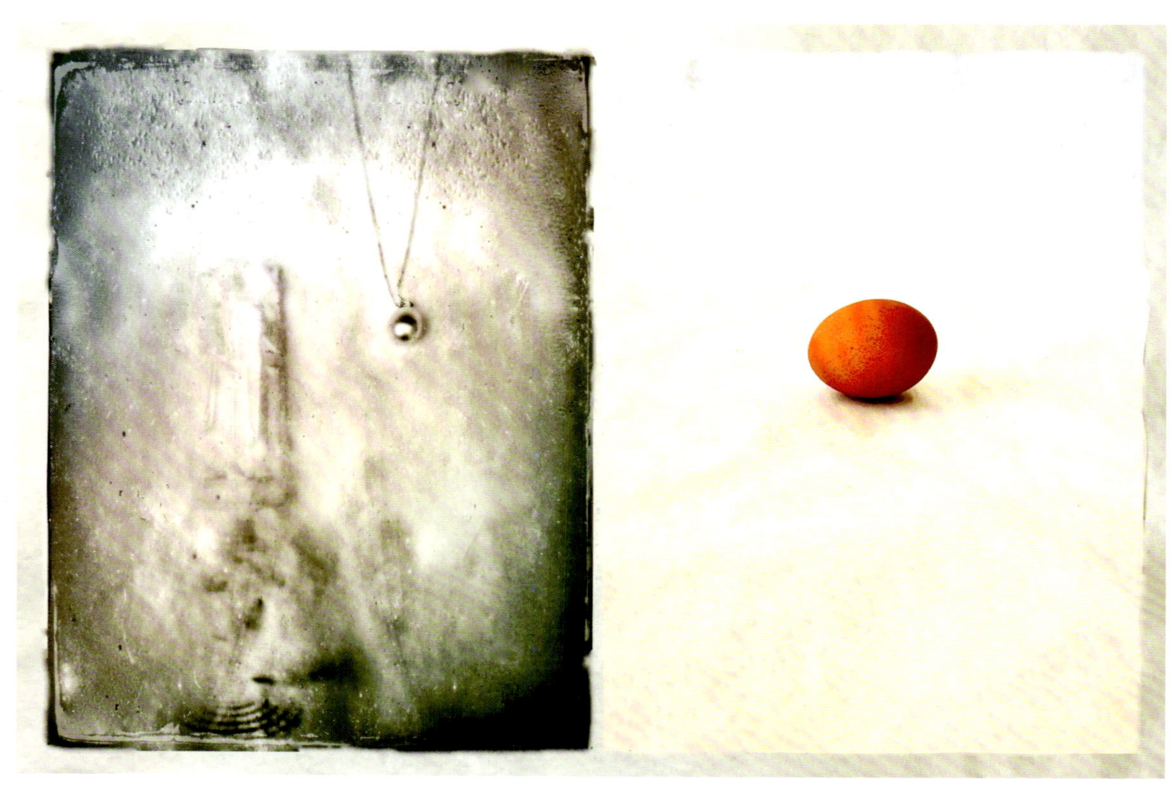

"A red egg, now that's a wonder," said the chess king.

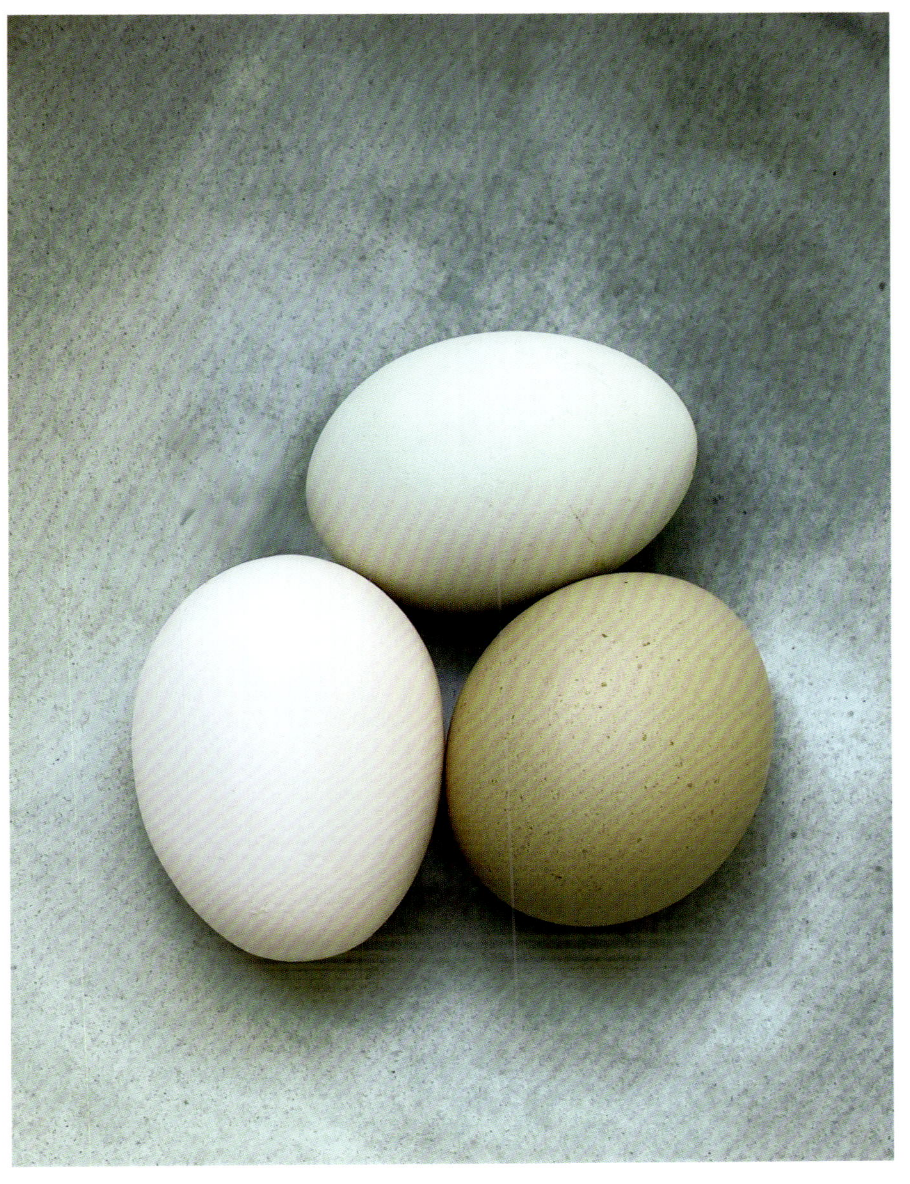

Eggs may have come first, but did they have any idea what they would hatch?

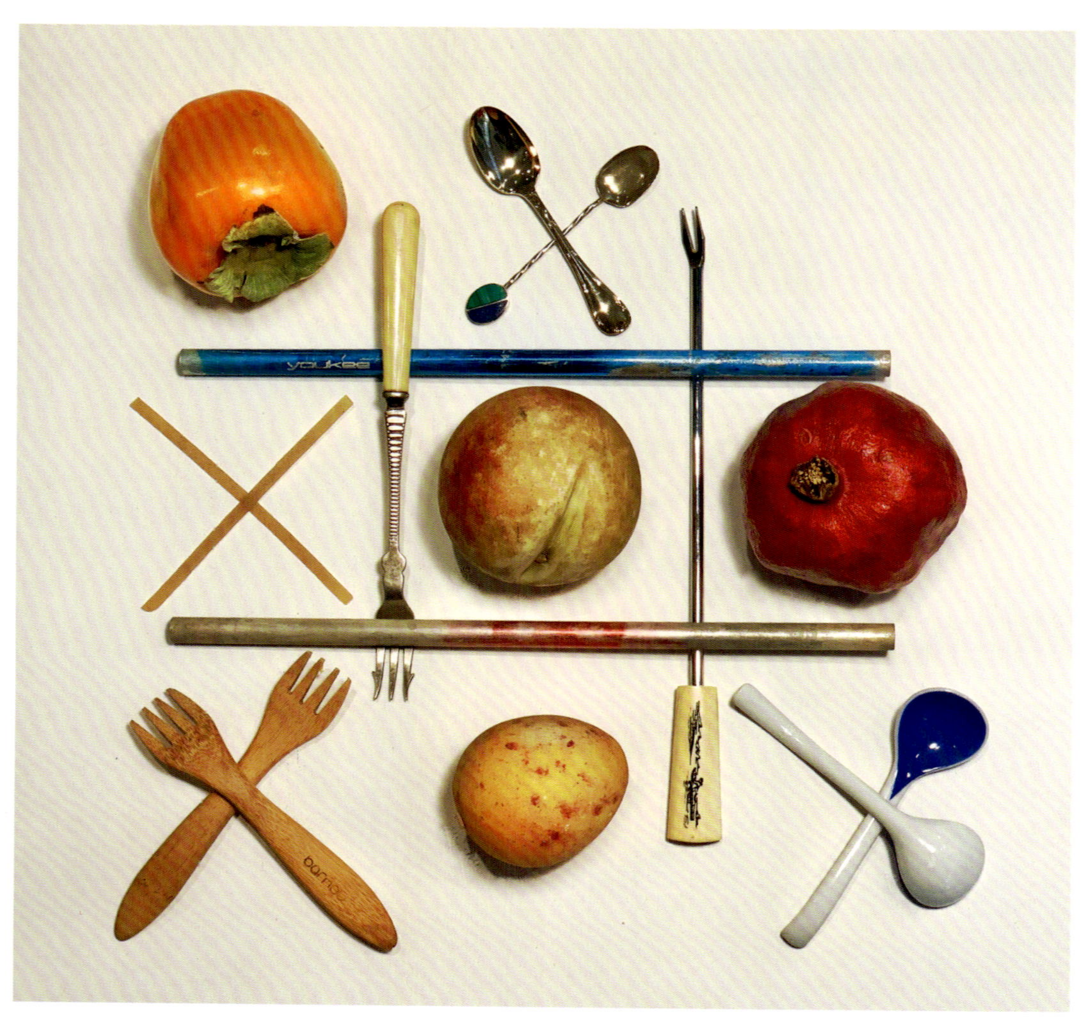

Choose your adversary carefully. Construct the playing board of useful objects.
Take turns making your moves.

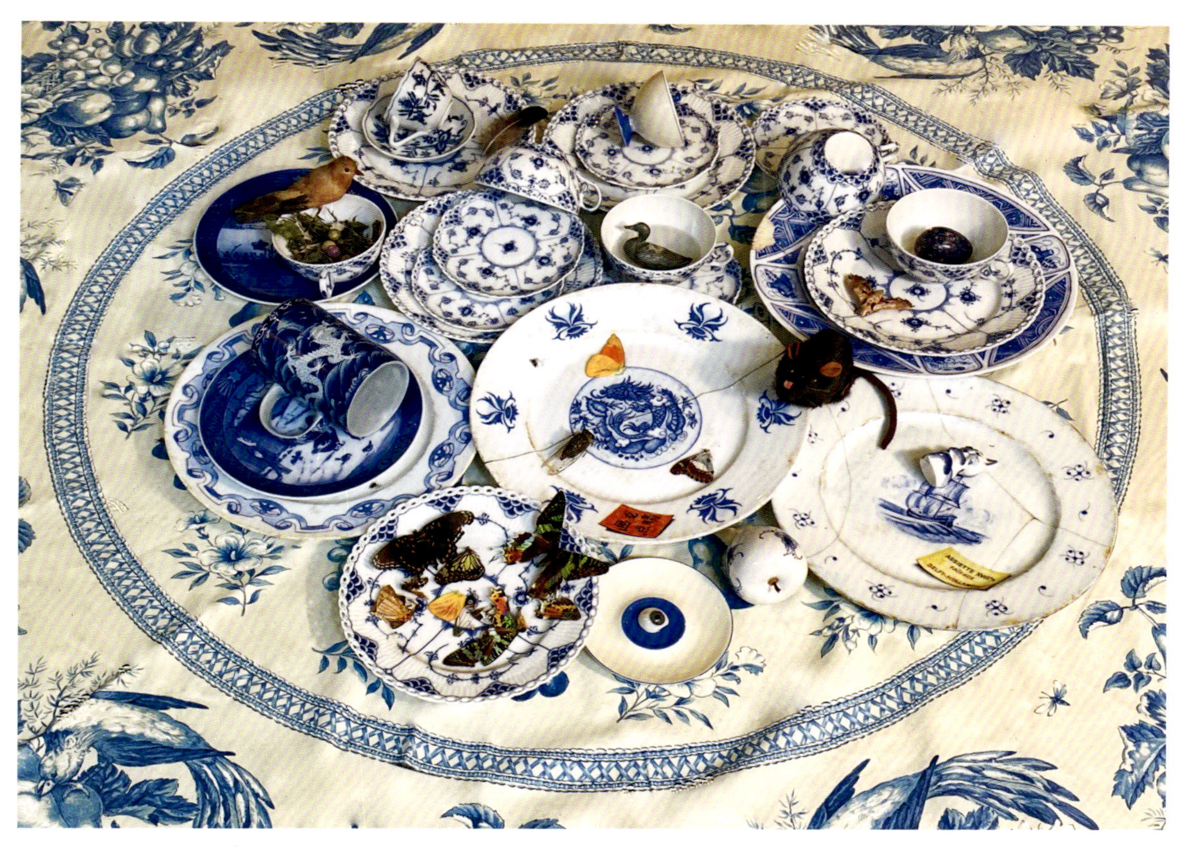

The wild creatures in you may growl, sting, or even gnaw at you,
but they will not play with you until you agree that civilization is flawed.

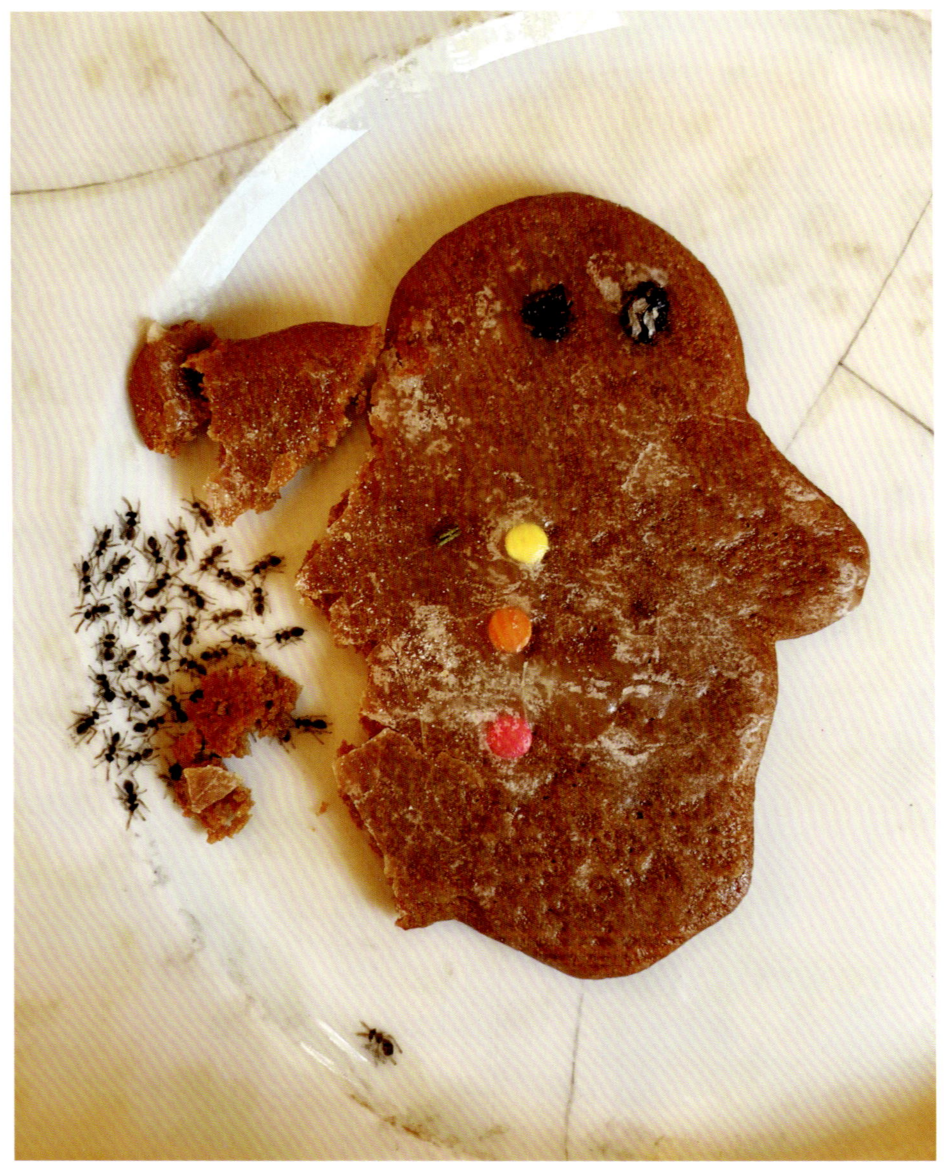

"To be or not to be?" Ants answered his question.

—hand-painted plate, Pierre Ducordeau, c. 1994

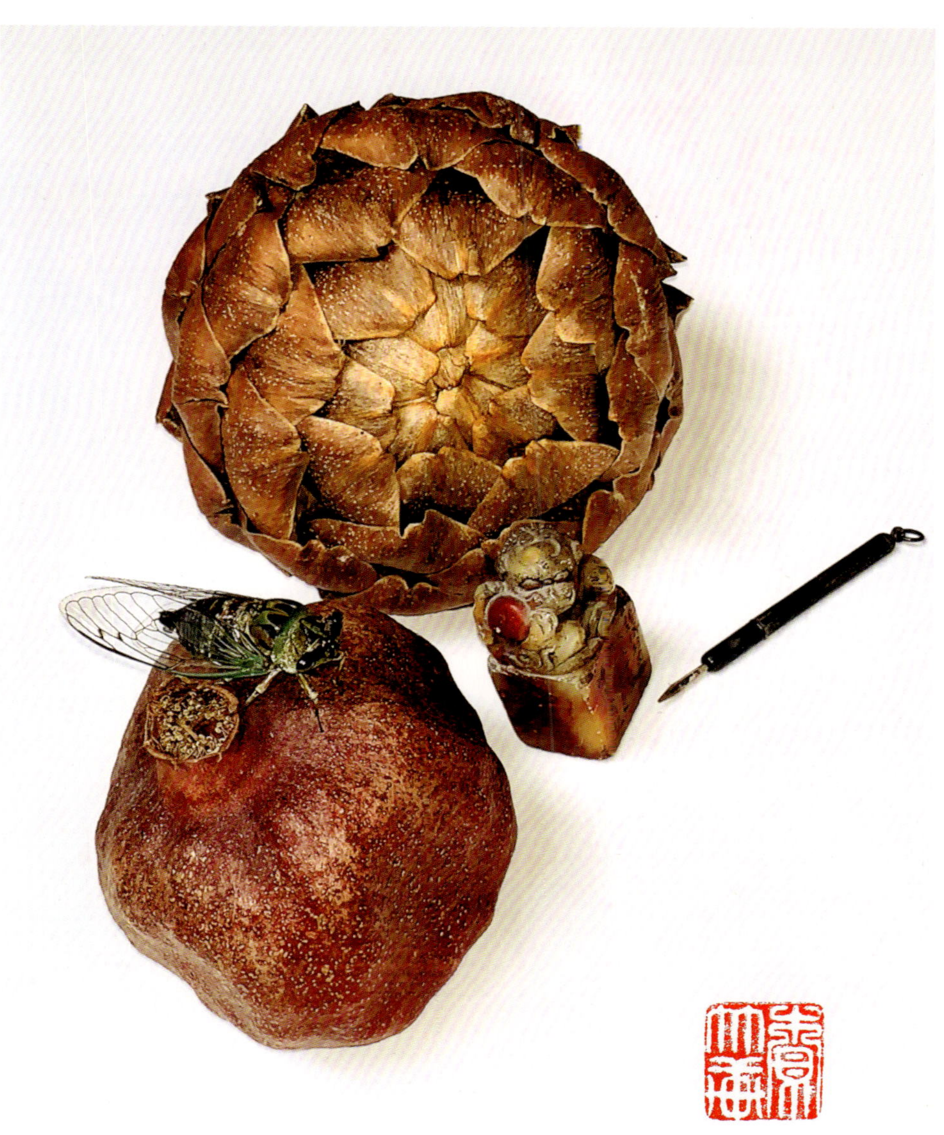

Objects have presence, heft and depth—color, form, reasons for being.
Everything has been here for a very long time.

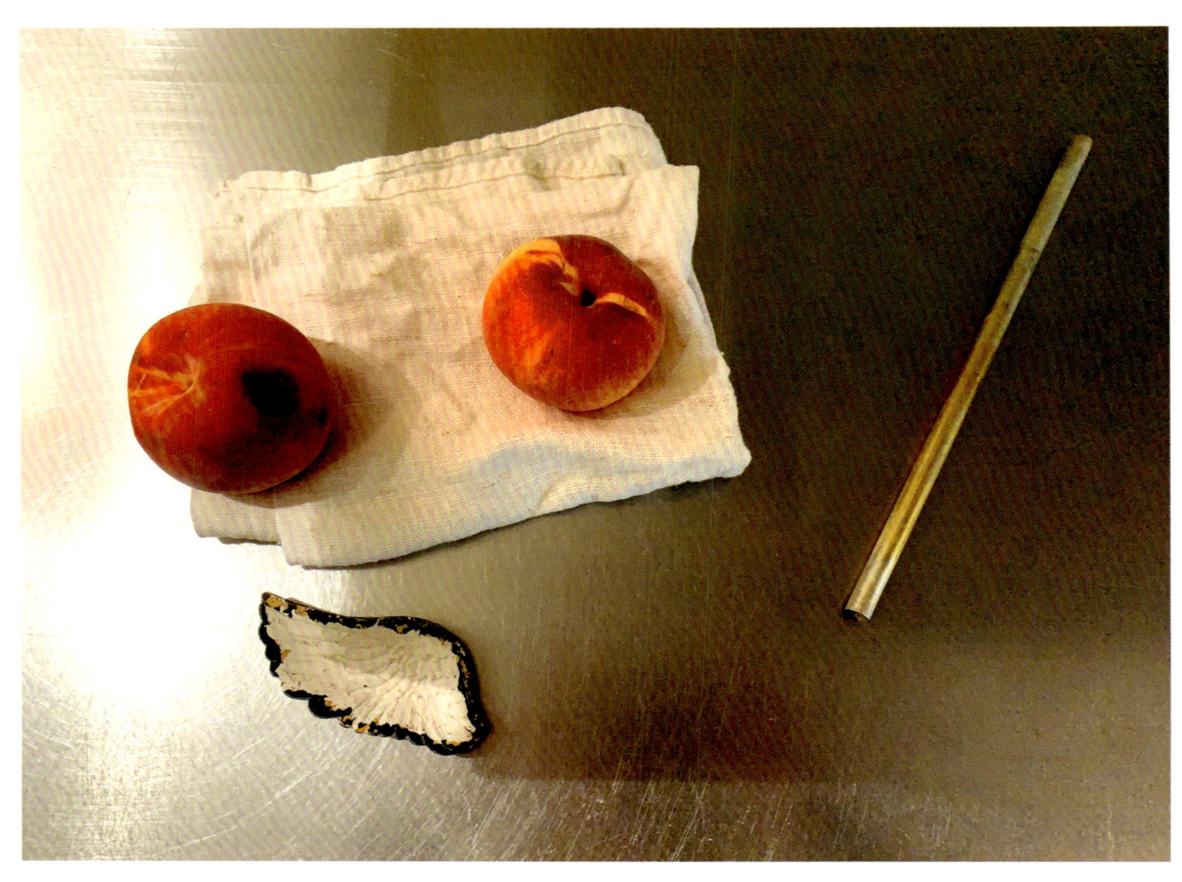

Still life titled *Peaches on a Kitchen Counter*.

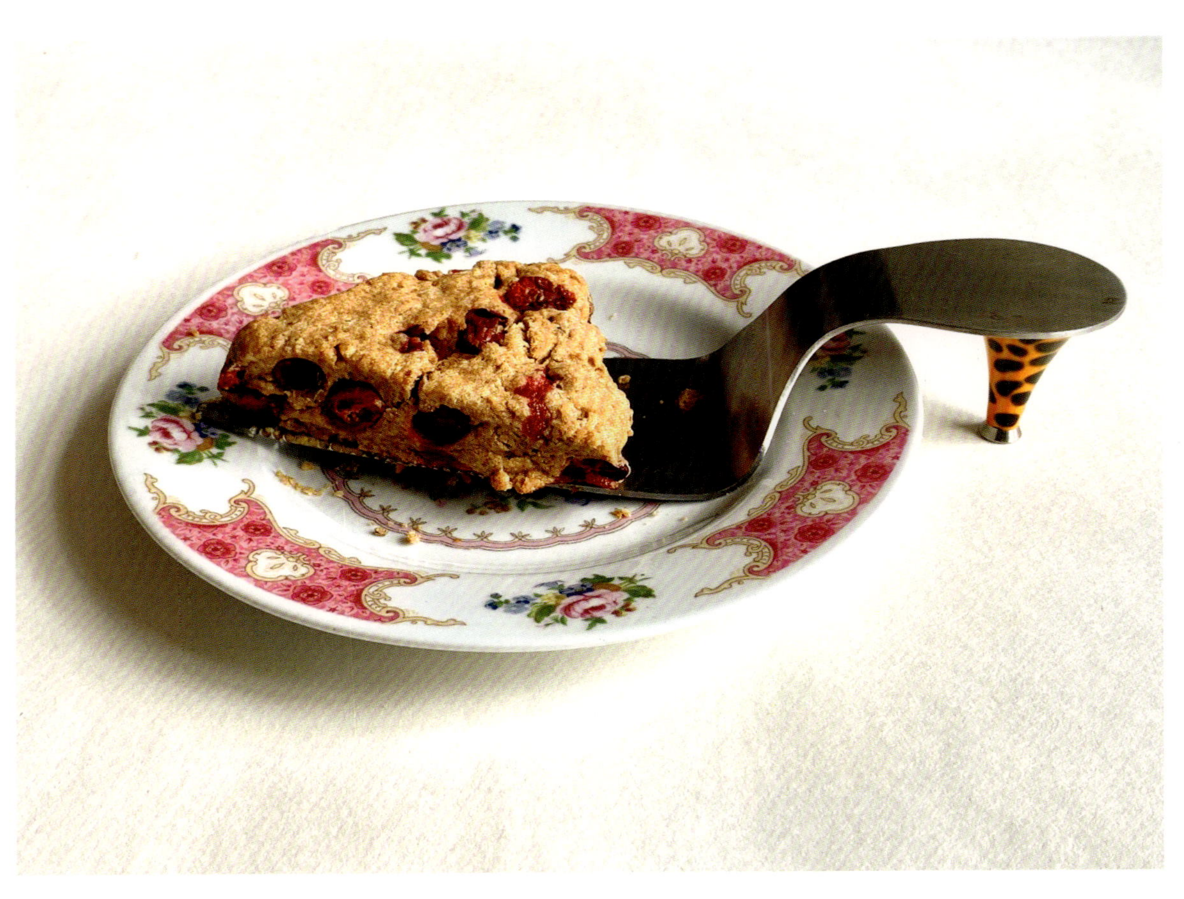

Her taste in scones and shoes runs toward the tart.

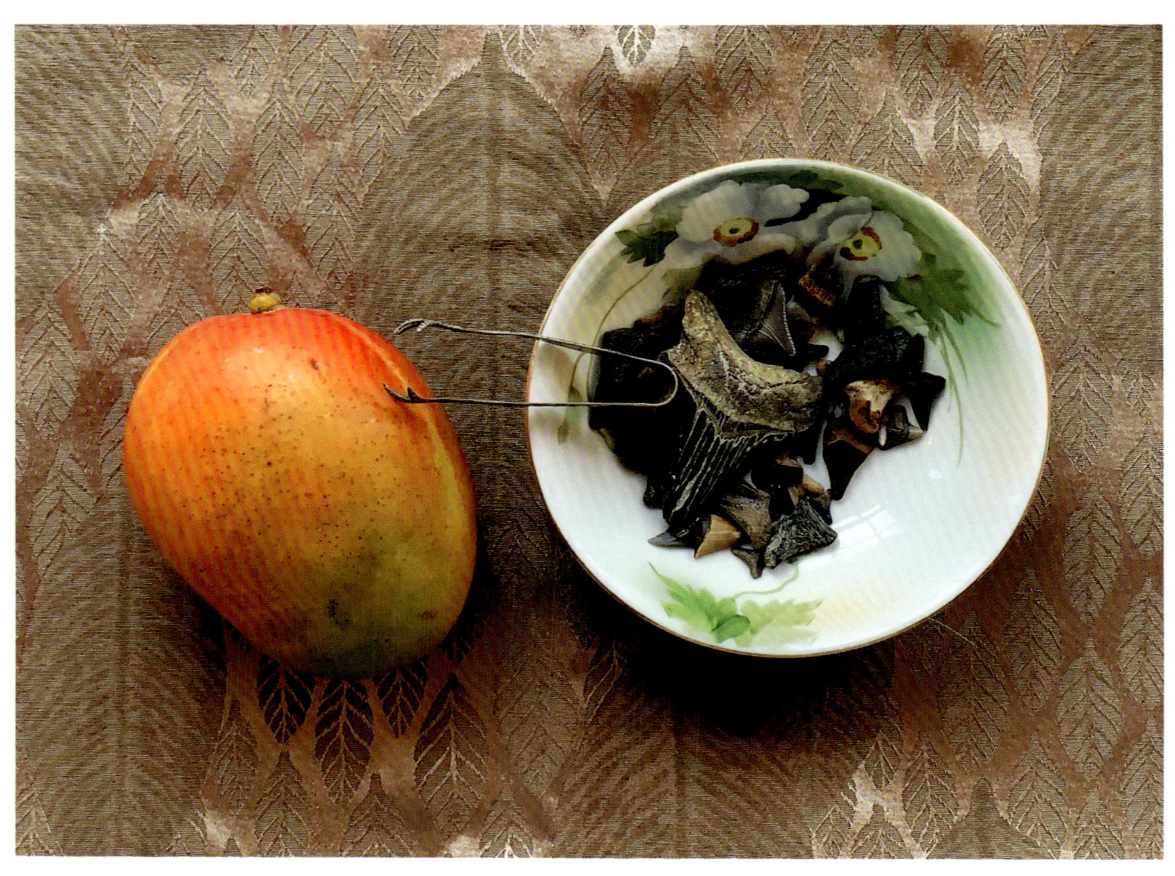

He gathered shark teeth fossils along the shore,
never knowing they came from lands where mangoes grew.

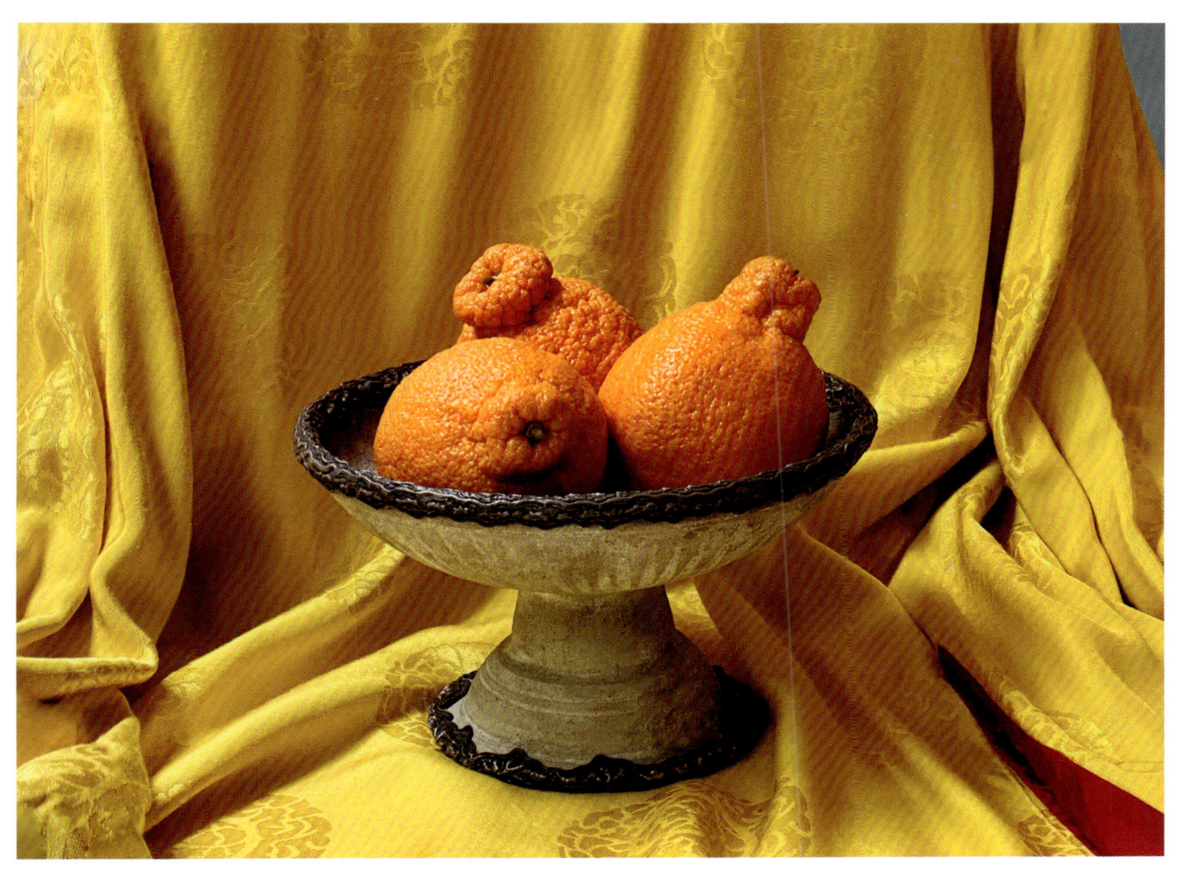

Oranges in an ancient Chinese bowl rung round with silver.
Their juice will run down our chins.

She looked me in the eye and said,
"The book got me out of my bubble. Thank you, I love it."

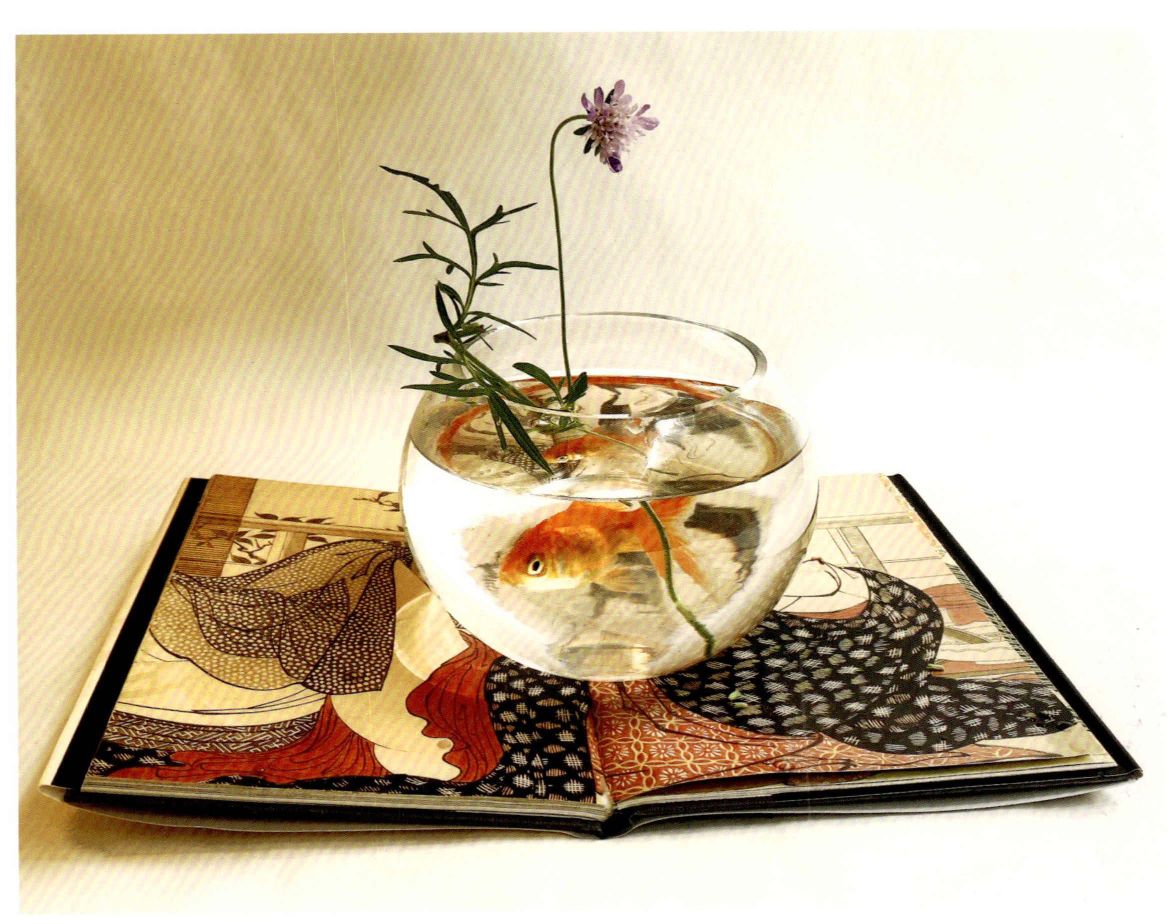

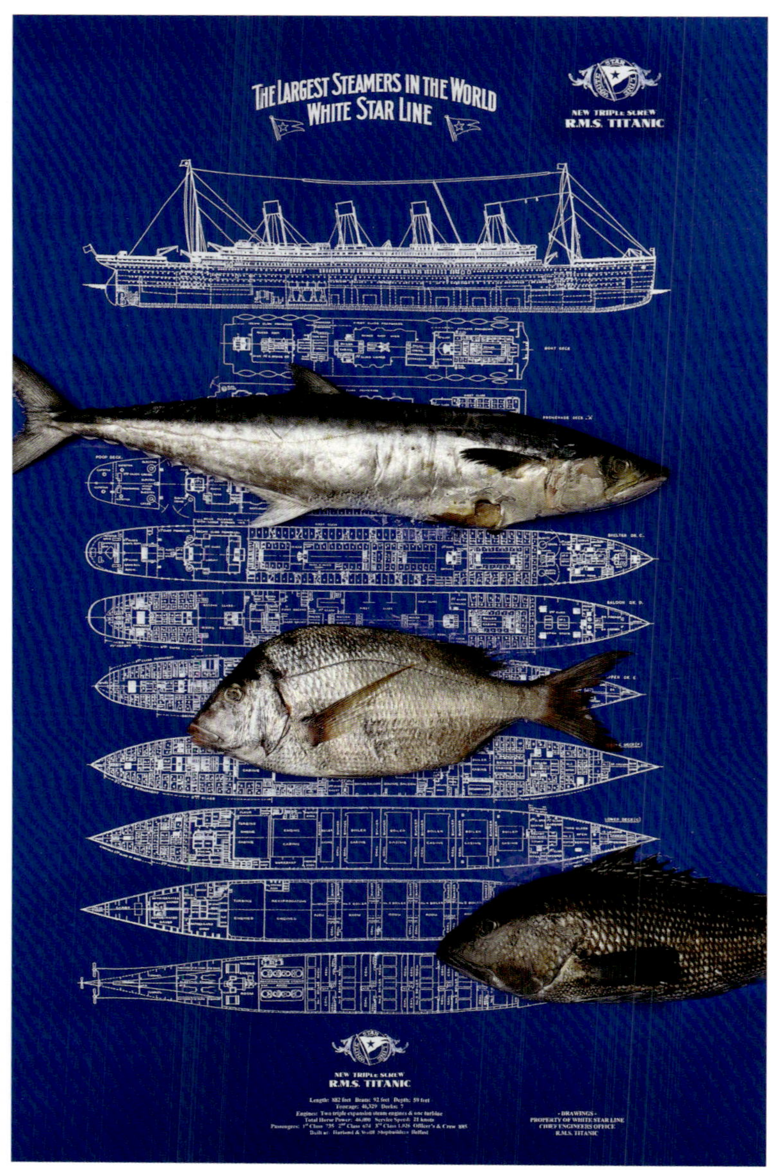

Sea creatures found homes in the invasion from above—
trumpets, china, mirrors, hard things, shiny things. Gifts from gods or a doomed species?
They did not try to understand. They occupied.

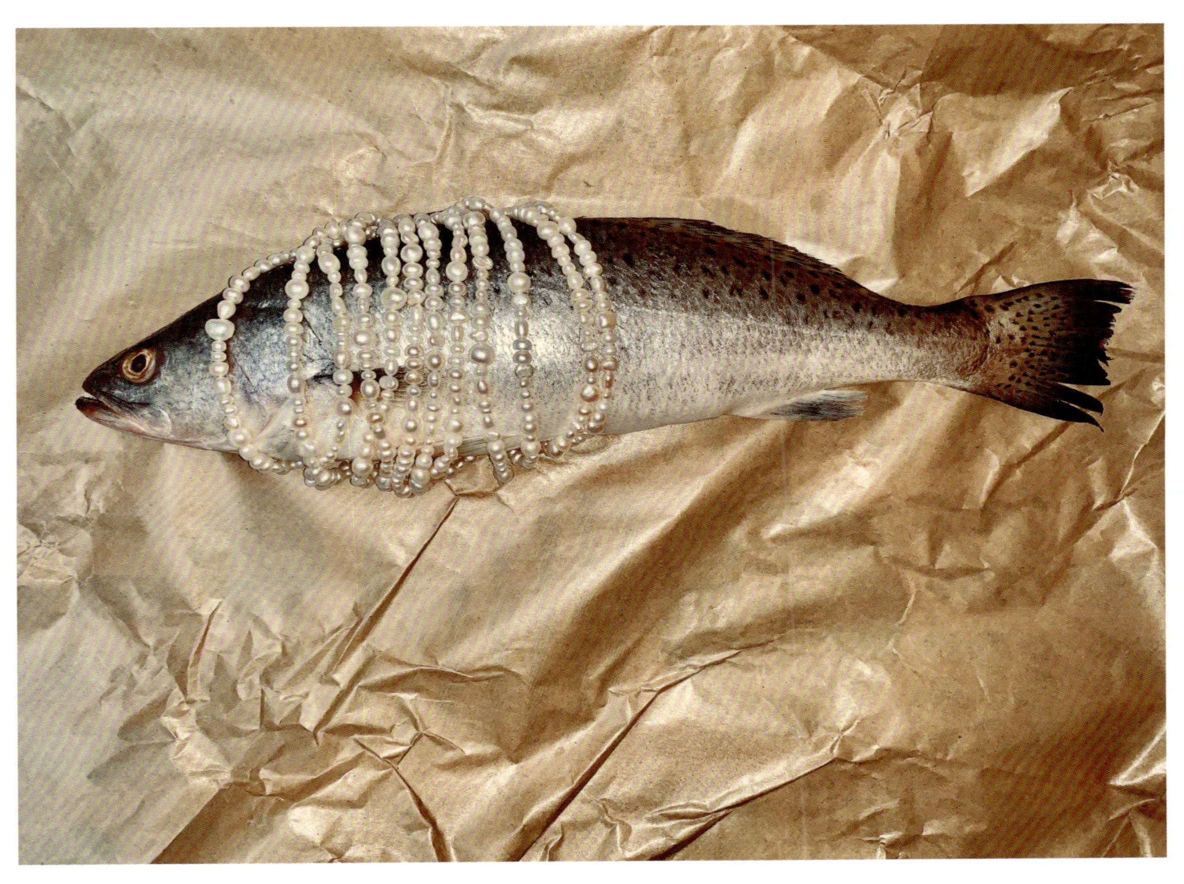

This is not a fish wrapped in pearls lying on brown paper.
It is a photographic moment of a fish that did not get away.

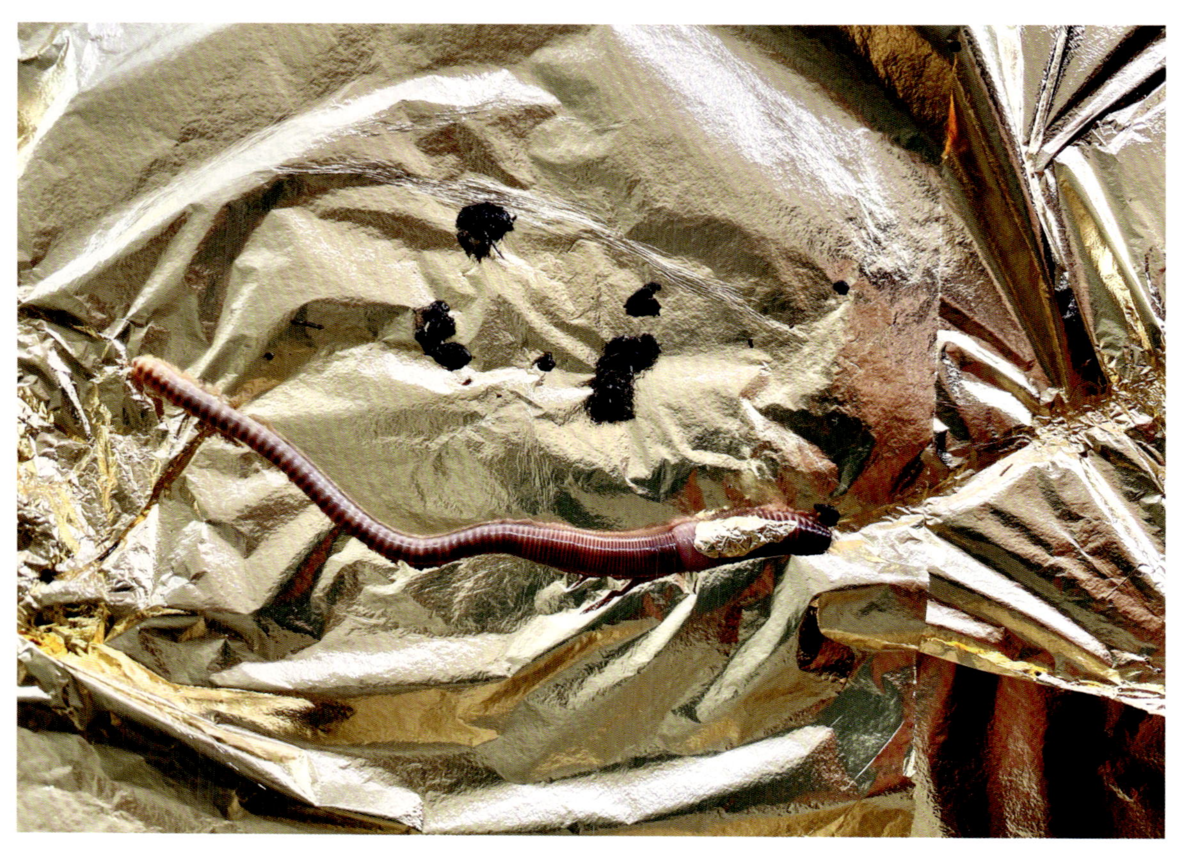

Gold? No, no. Worms know dirt is best.

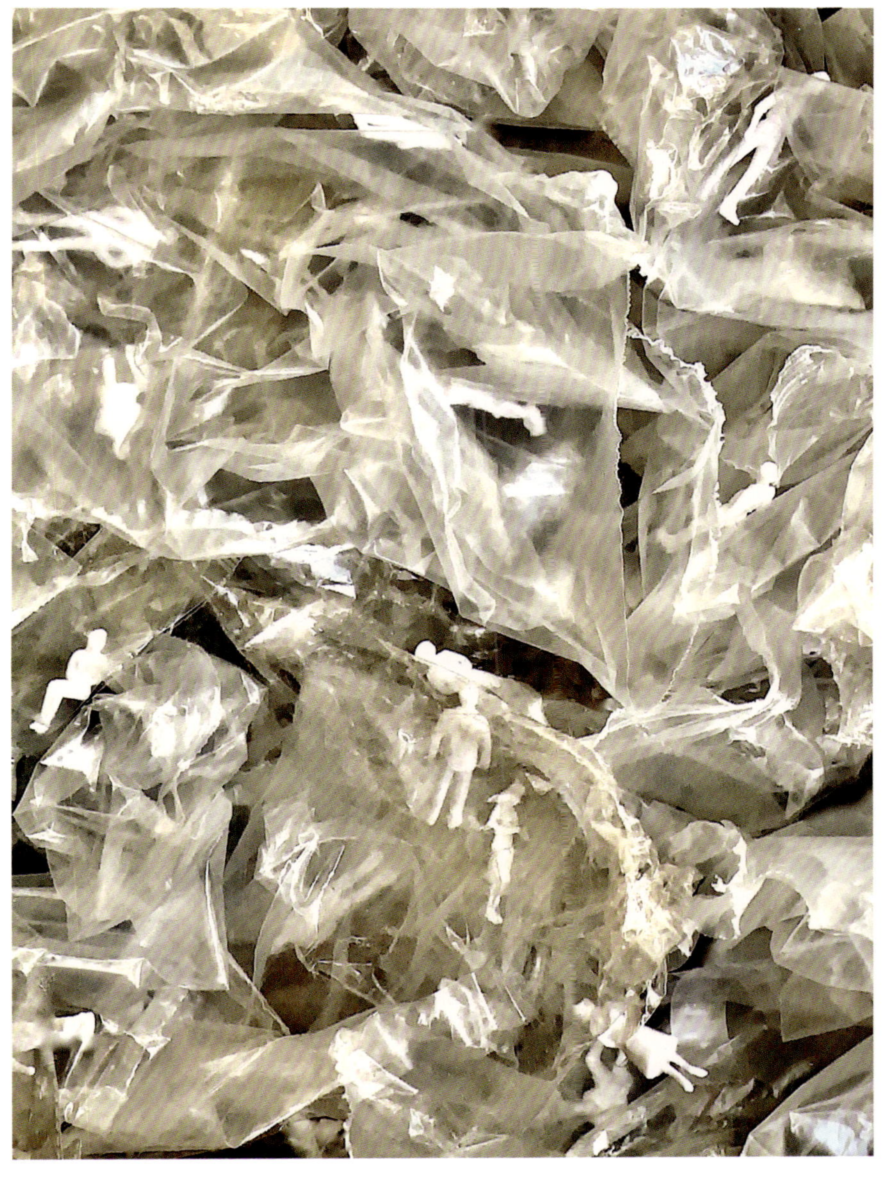

Pull back and see what we have done, plastic death raking in lush and green.
Now, get in close and clean it up.

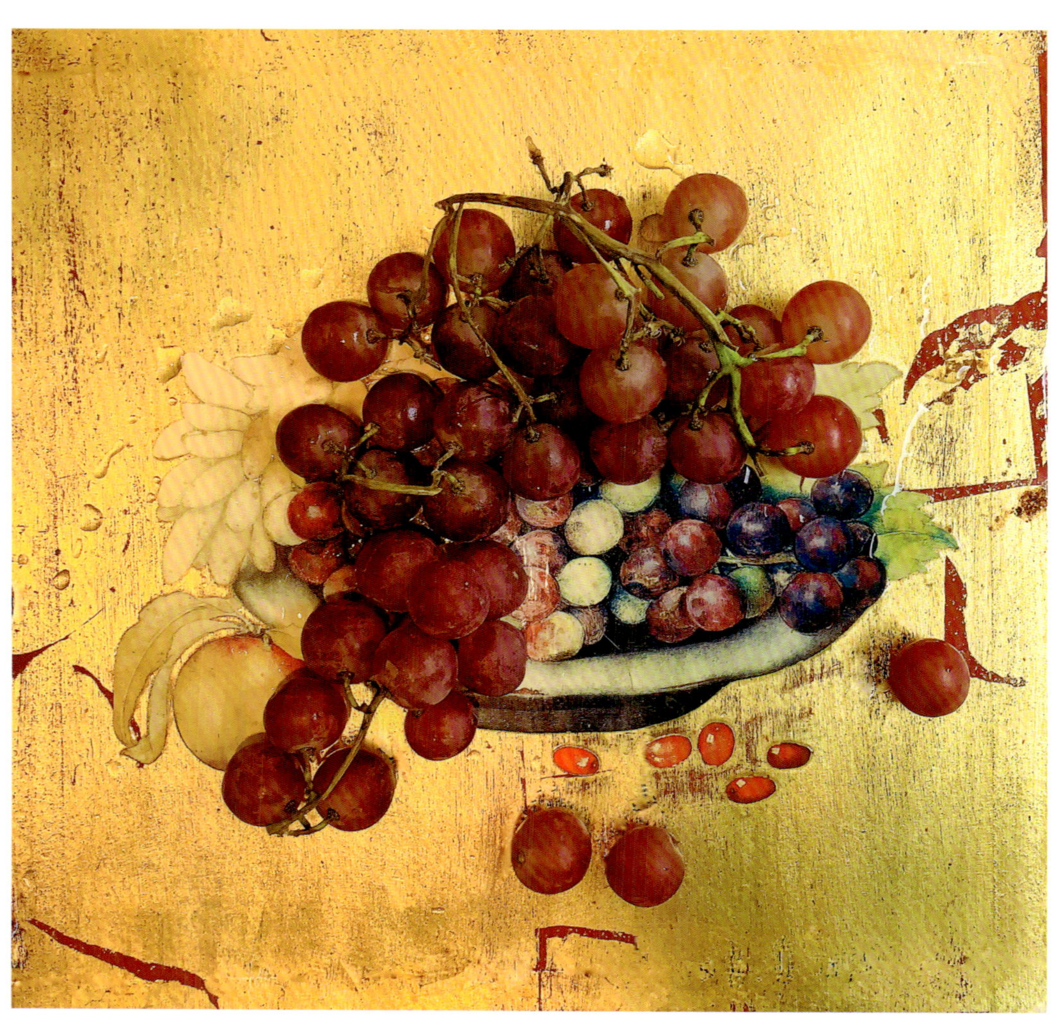

Many fruits are illogical—grapes among the most.

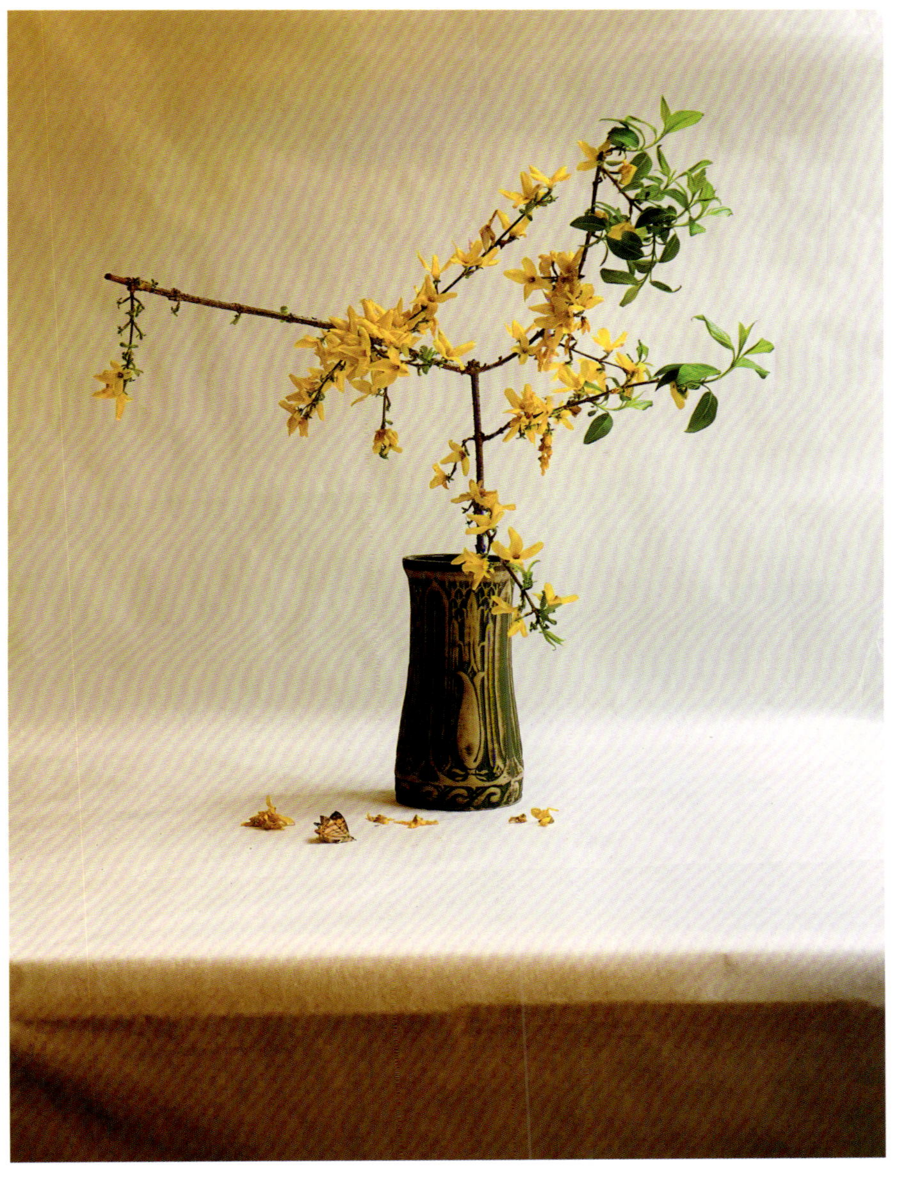

The best beauty is disjointed. It has mystery, a falling off, a hint of what was and what will be, or might be, or never will be except in a knowing inside of us.

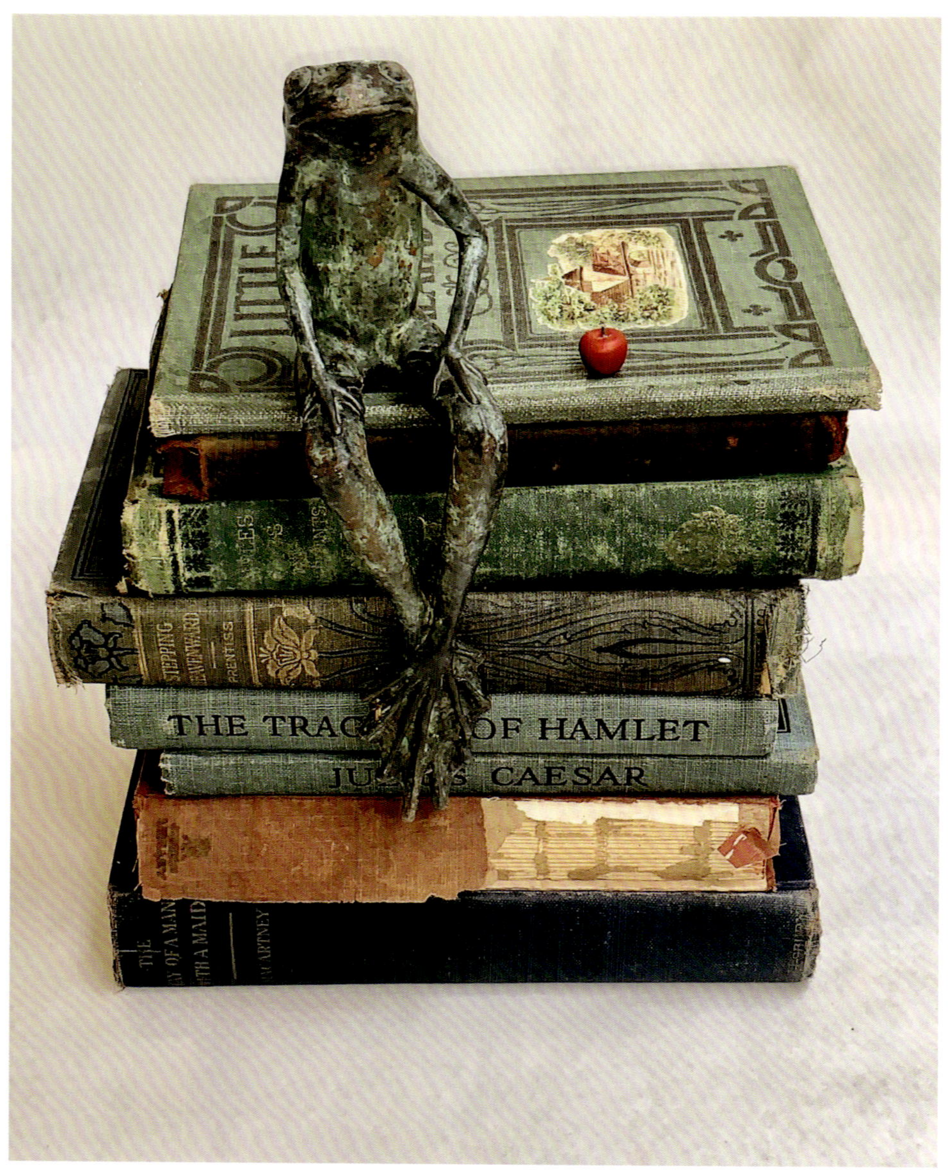

The years of waiting for her kiss grew long and the romance of the idea grew stale, so he turned to logic and became a scholar of the great tragedies.

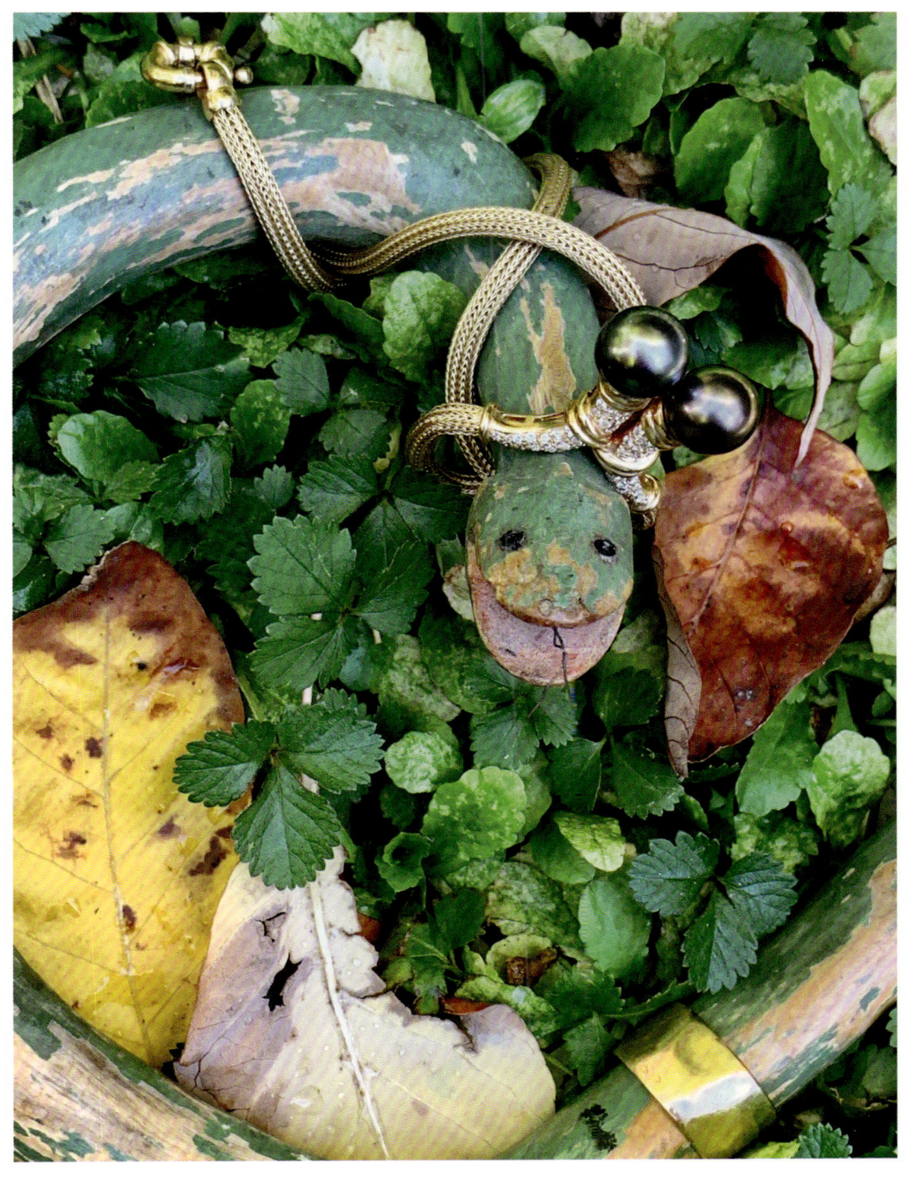

All dressed up and no one to bite.

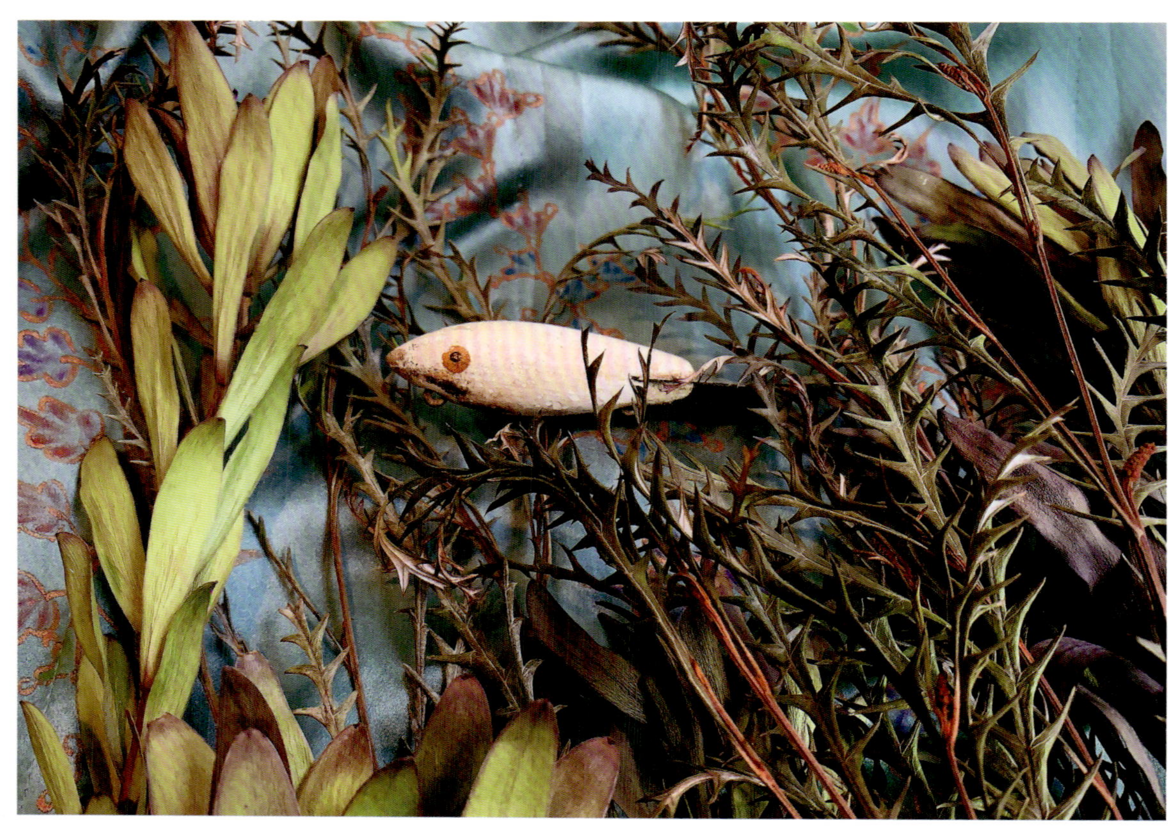

The strange little fish, weary of being teased, left school to swim in oceans of silk and dreams.

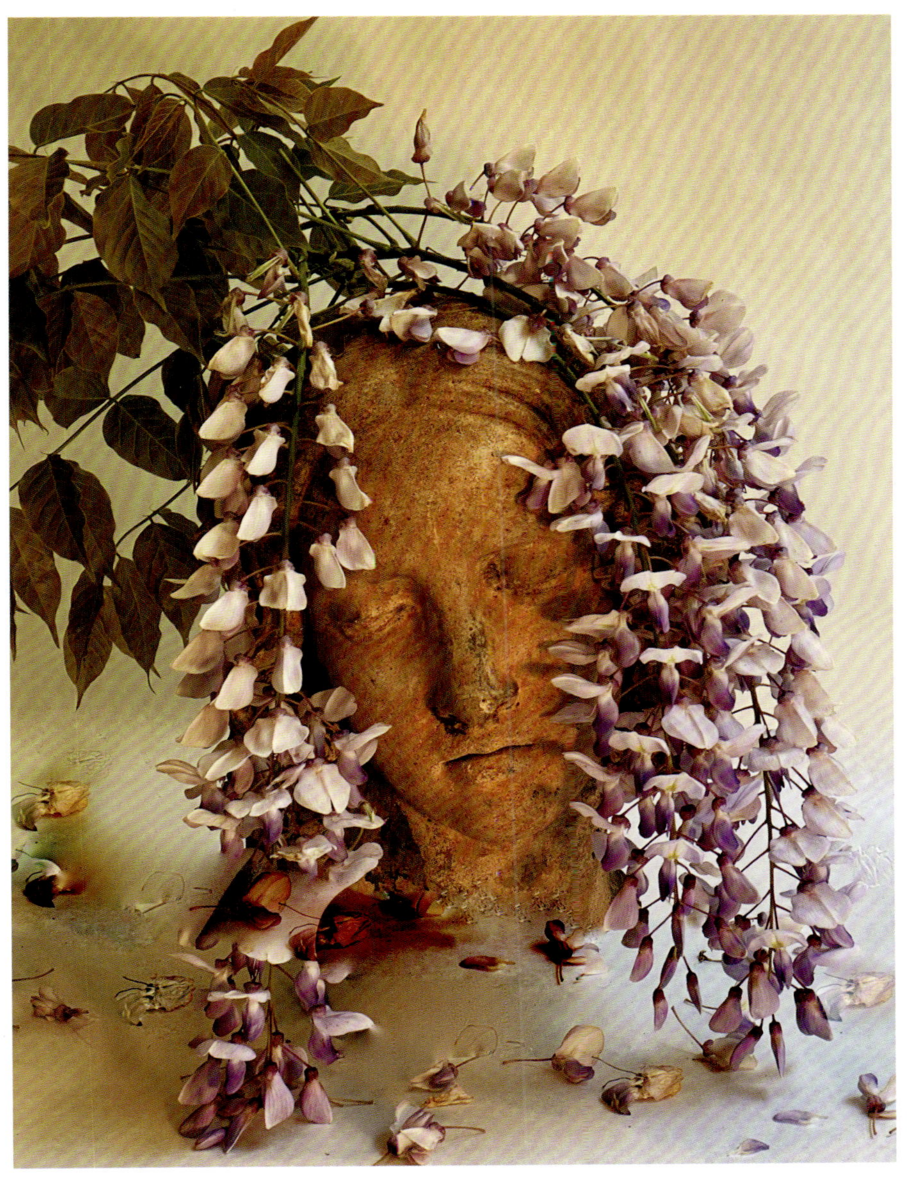

Wisteria salved his melancholy.

—terracotta bust, French

She arrived with no job, no place to stay, and one suitcase,
so she went immediately to the National Gallery of Art where, rounding a corner,
she saw Odilon Redon's *Pandora*. Her knees gave way.

—detail of Pandora, *1914, now at Metropolitan Museum of Art, NYC, with quail eggs*

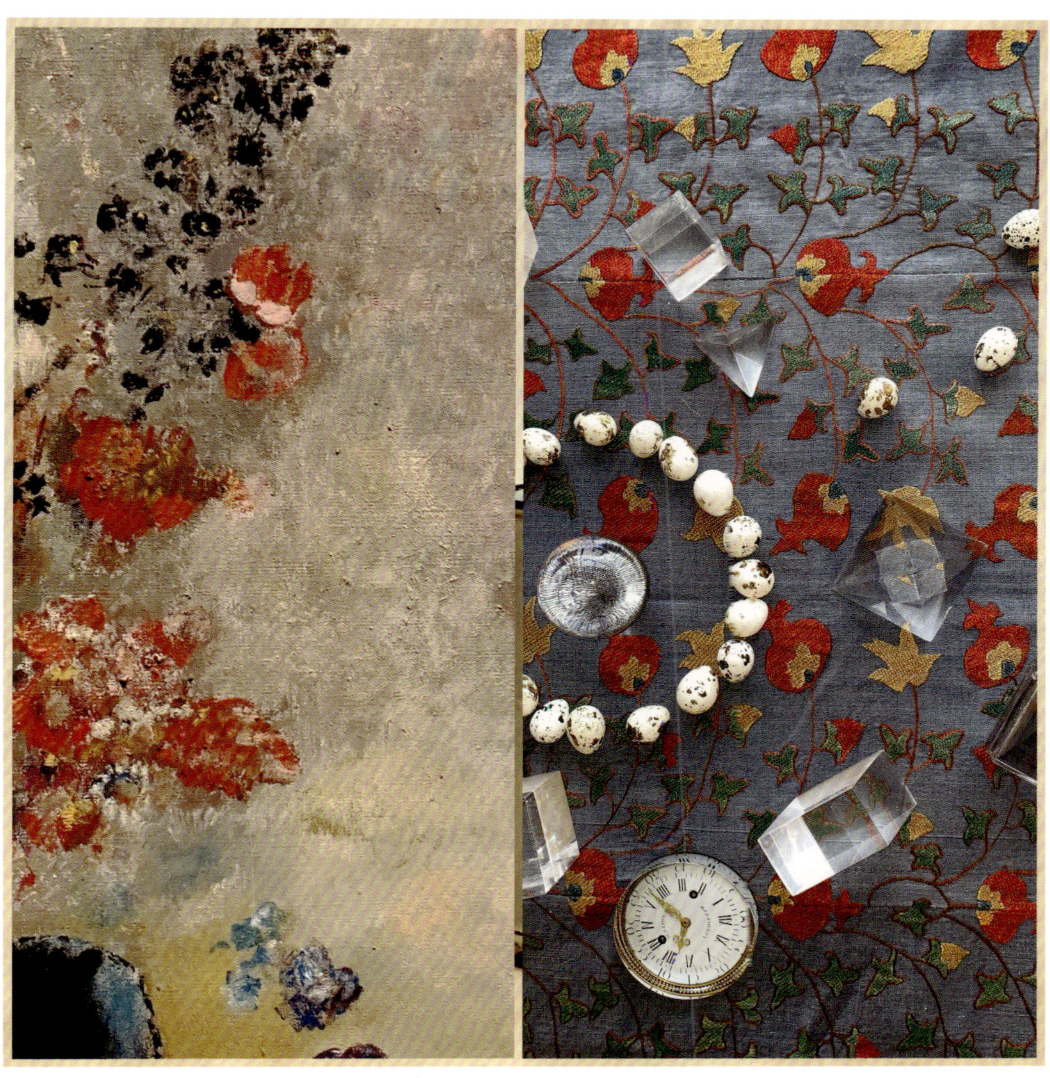

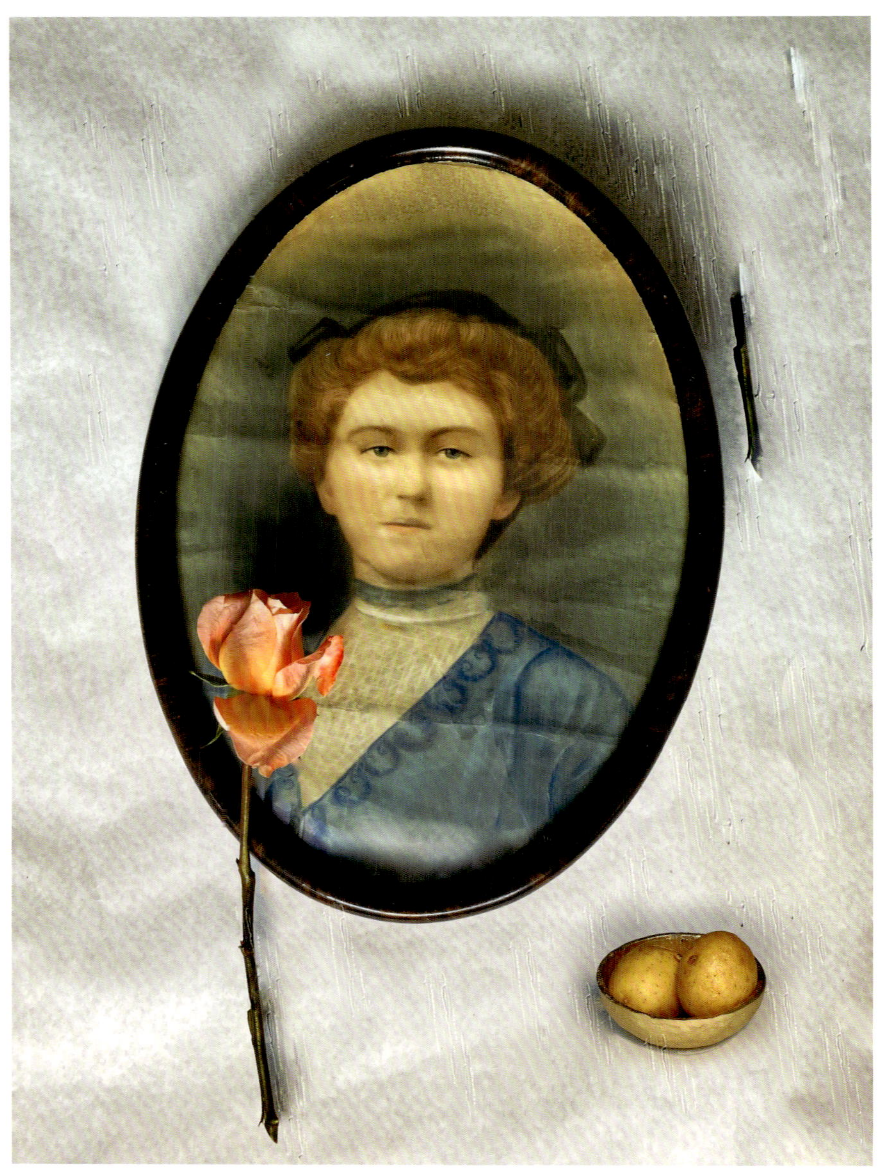

Lyda Rose spent half her life peeling and boiling potatoes for six children and a surly husband. Arthritis nearly crippled her but she stroked my cheek with the back of her gnarled hands.

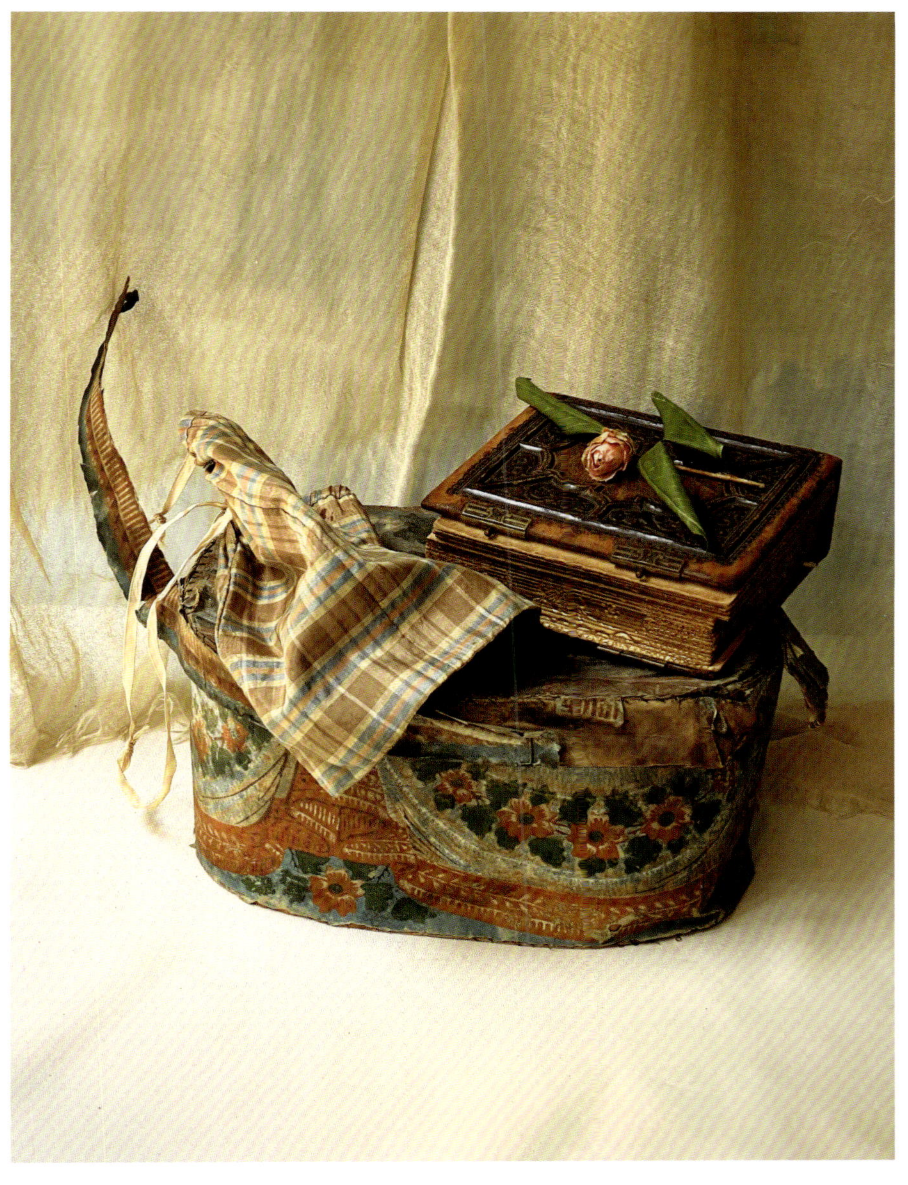

The dust in the attic was nearly overpowering, but I found your little hat box, the book, and the silk bag. Where did the flower come from?

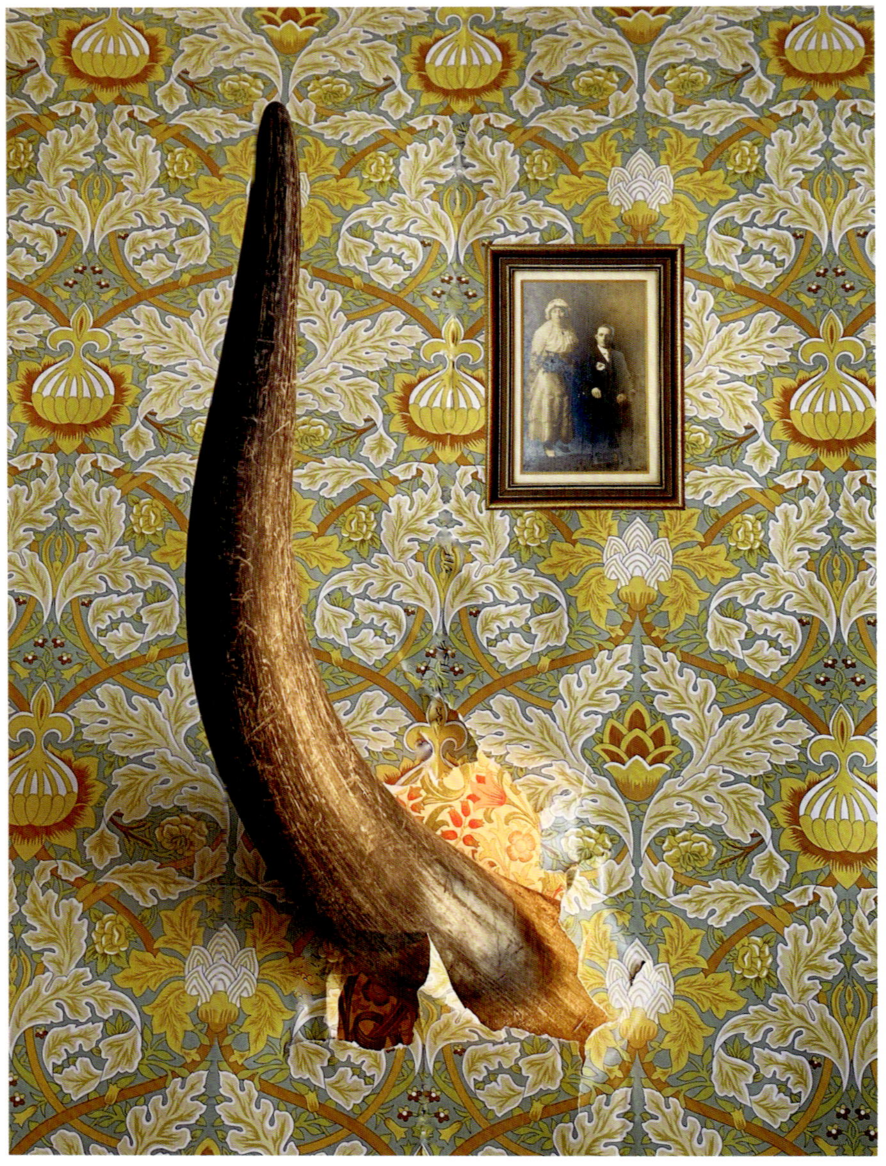

He died from a bad heart before turning 60 after lording it over her for 35 years.

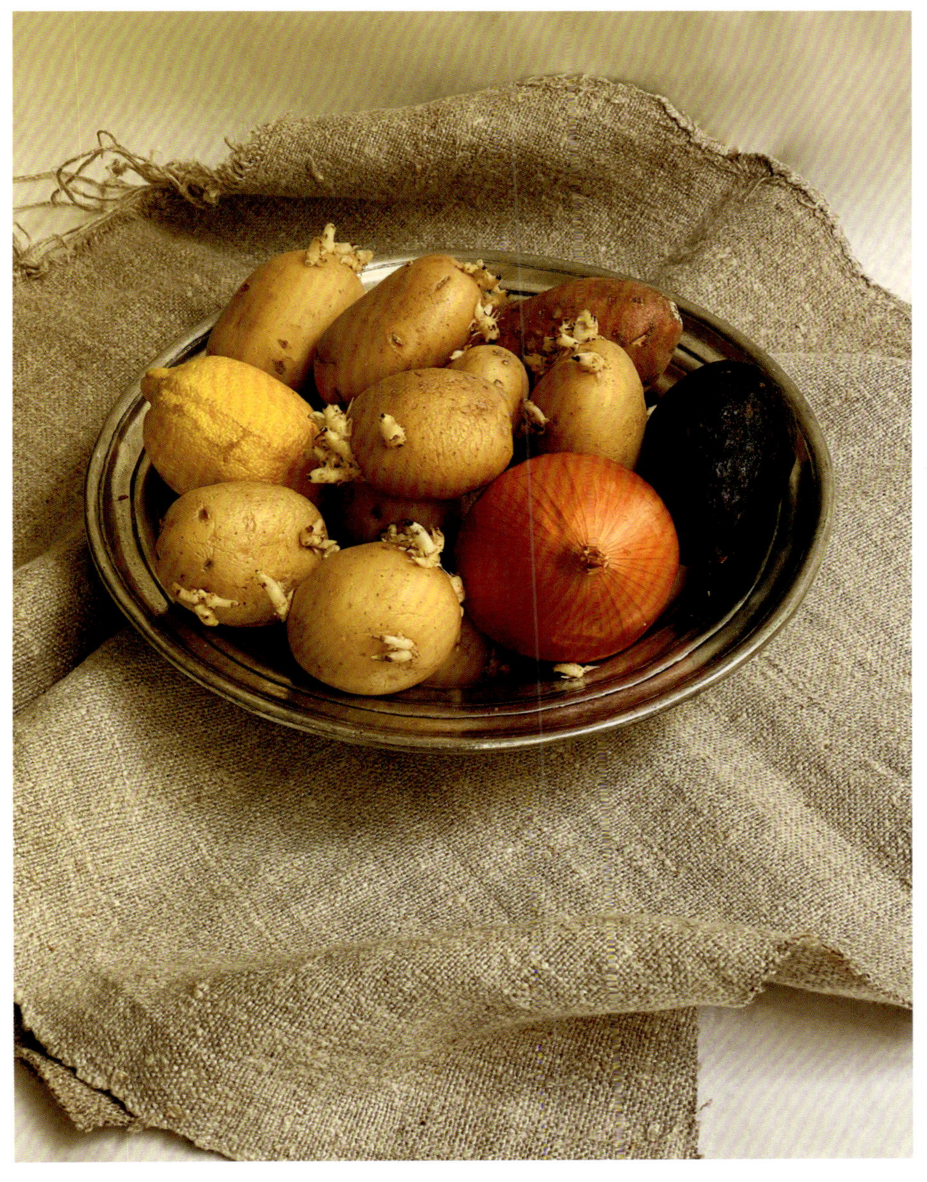

Easing into death was not so dark or lonely as she feared. It felt a returning, subsuming potatoes, lace on the backs of chairs, her children, and the gray hairs on her chin.

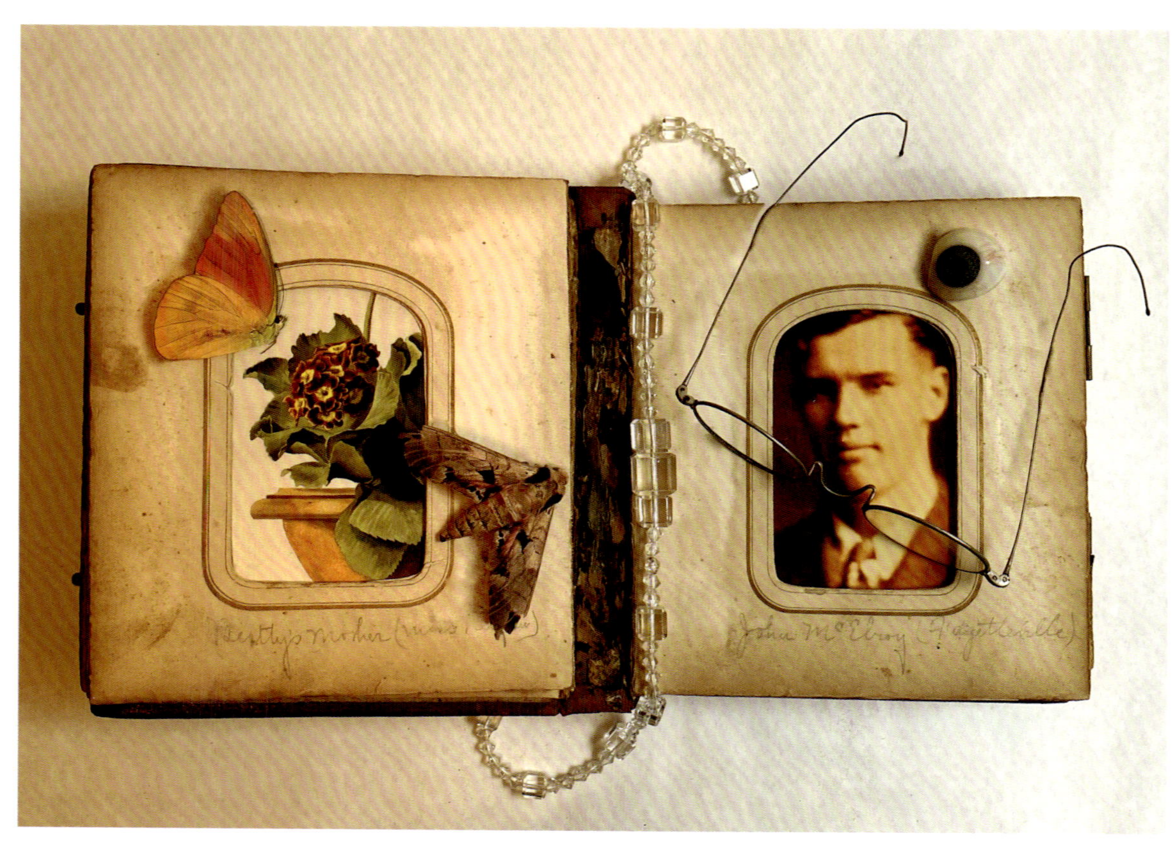

He was 34 and asleep on the front lawn when my mother drove up to ask directions to the one-room schoolhouse where she was assigned for the next year. She broke her vow never to marry a farmer.

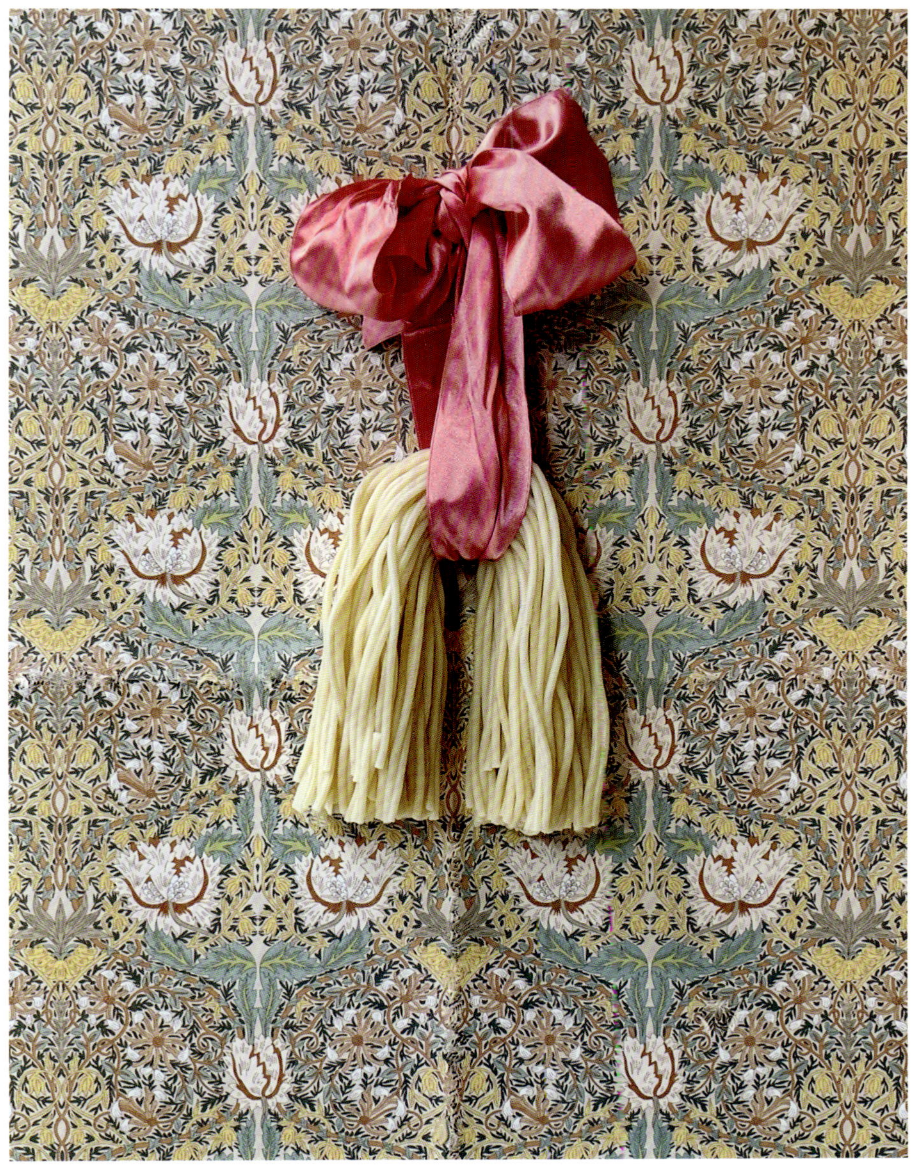

My aunt believed demons are blind when they look up, so she lived in the attic where she constructed a vanity table of orange crates and wrapped the edges of a broken mirror with pink satin, and sculpted clay busts of the Madonna.

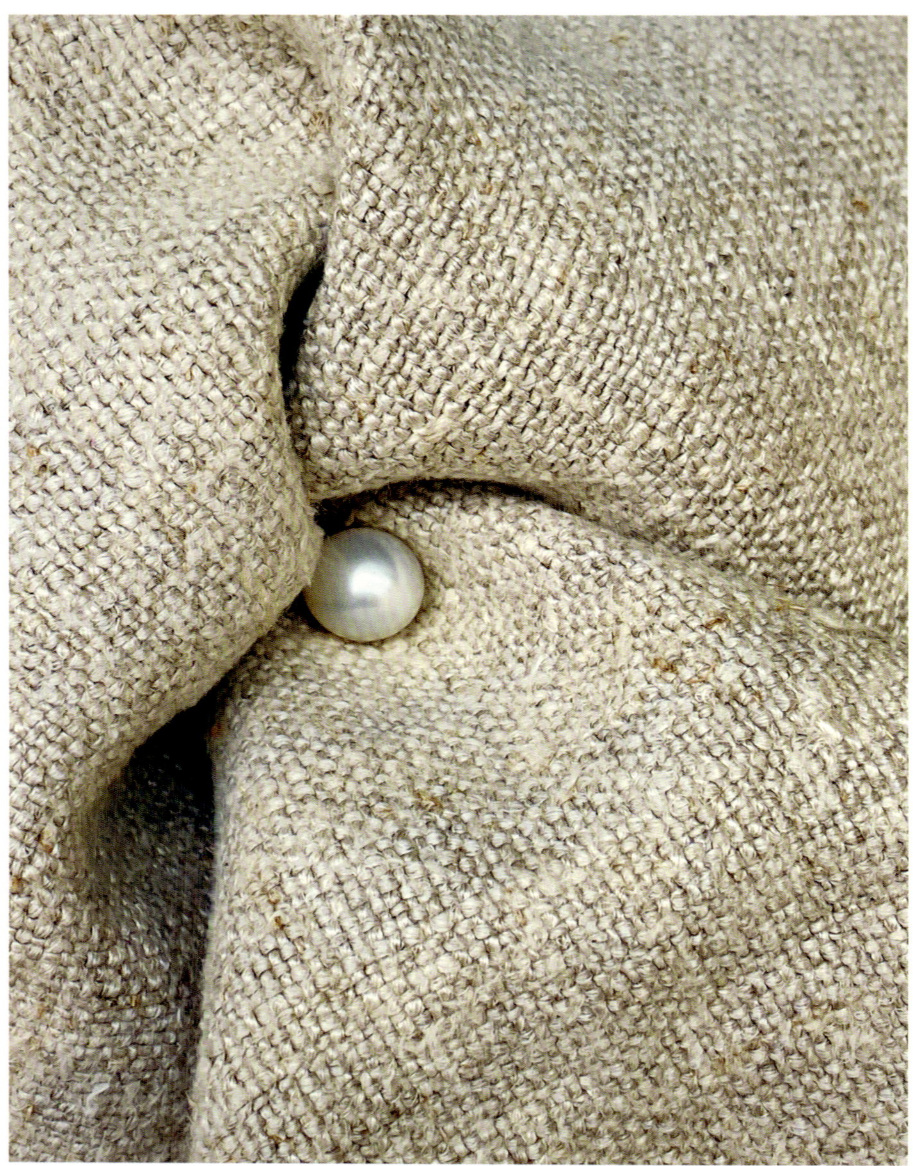

Do not presume you know what is held inside a harsh exterior.

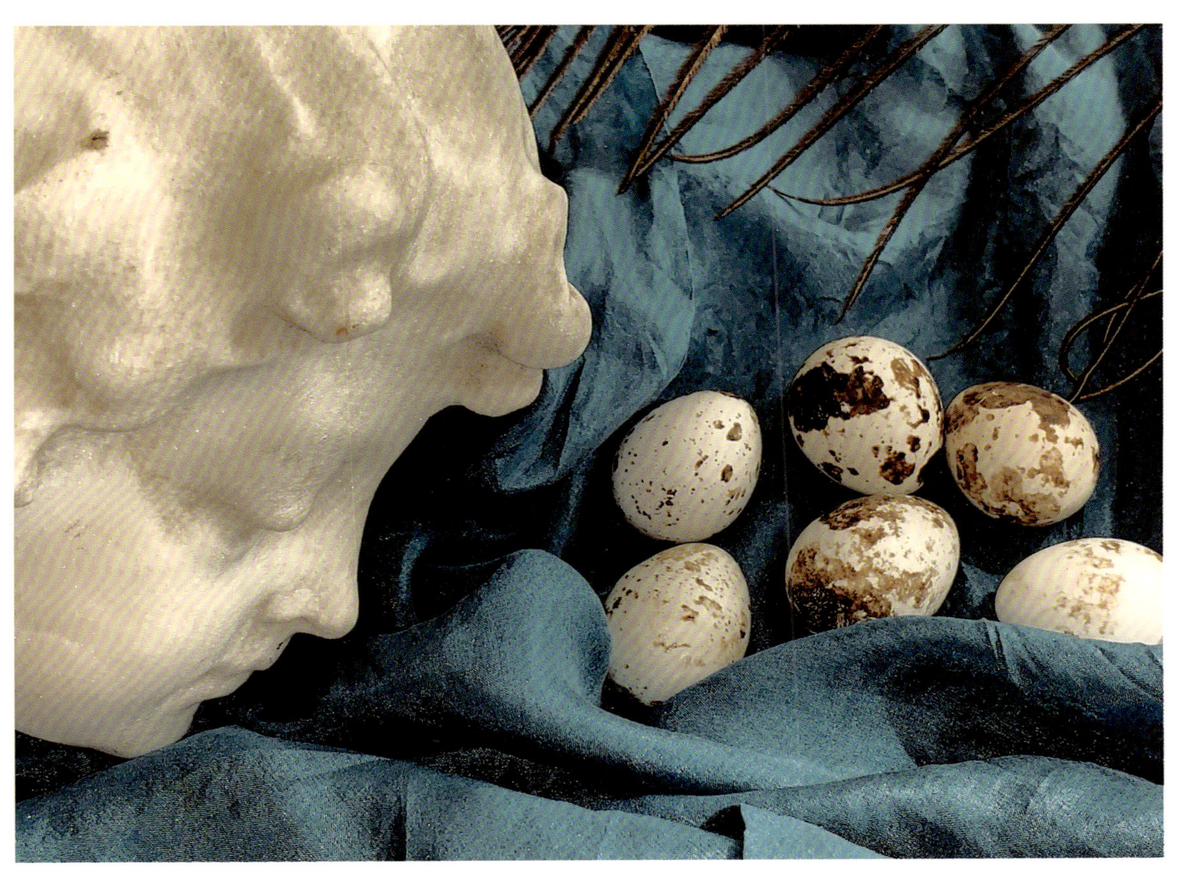

Vigilance only appears tender. It has conserved life since the beginning.

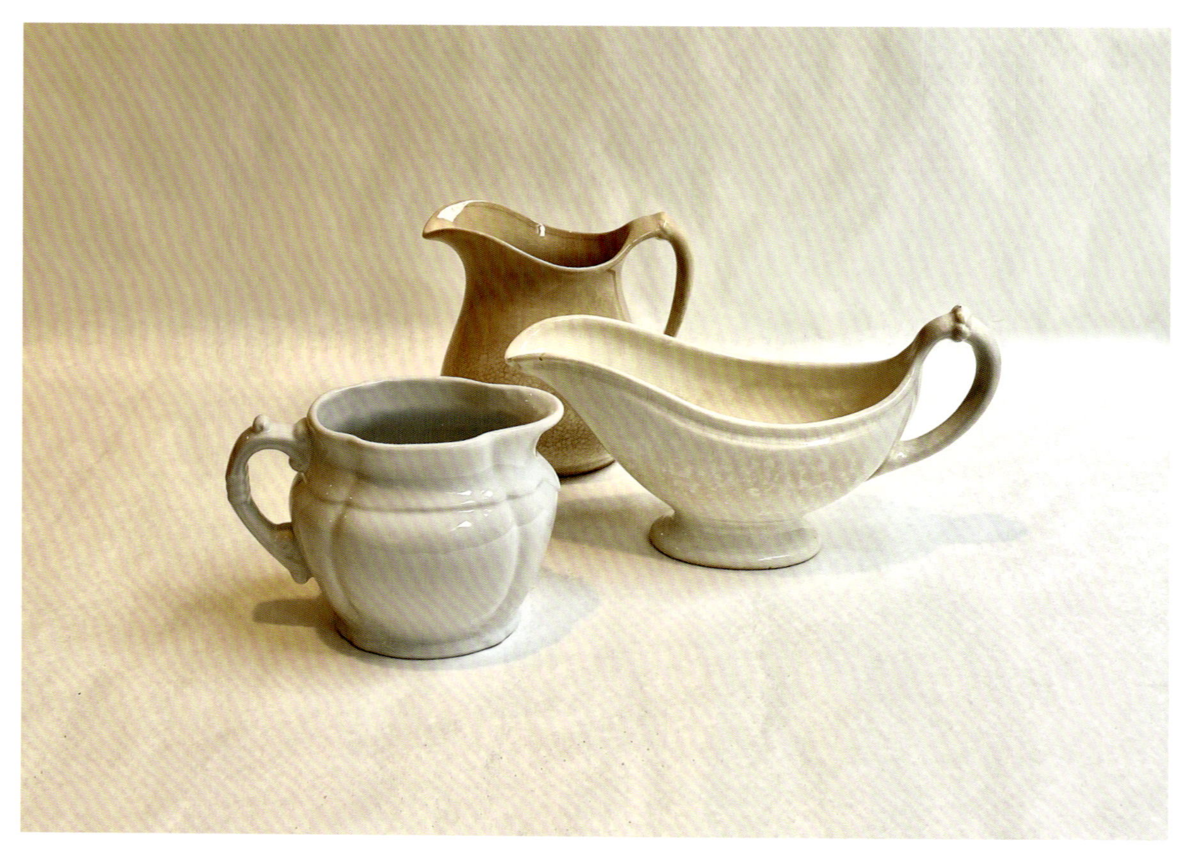

You need not speak of us. We are enough on our own.

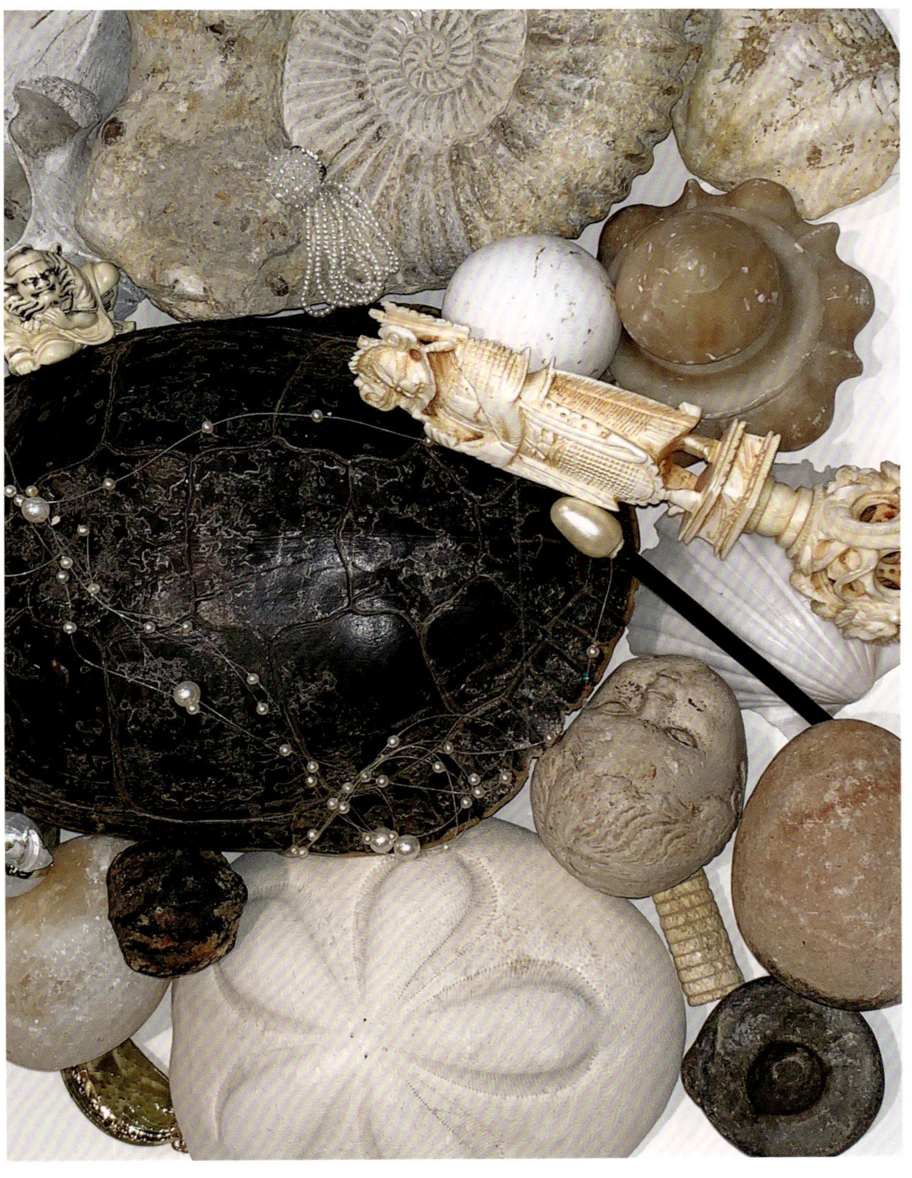

Colors tell you their stories, but blacks and whites call you inside them where you must listen well.

If you feel the pulse of the universe even once, you know bliss has no need of form.

—*velvet pincushion*

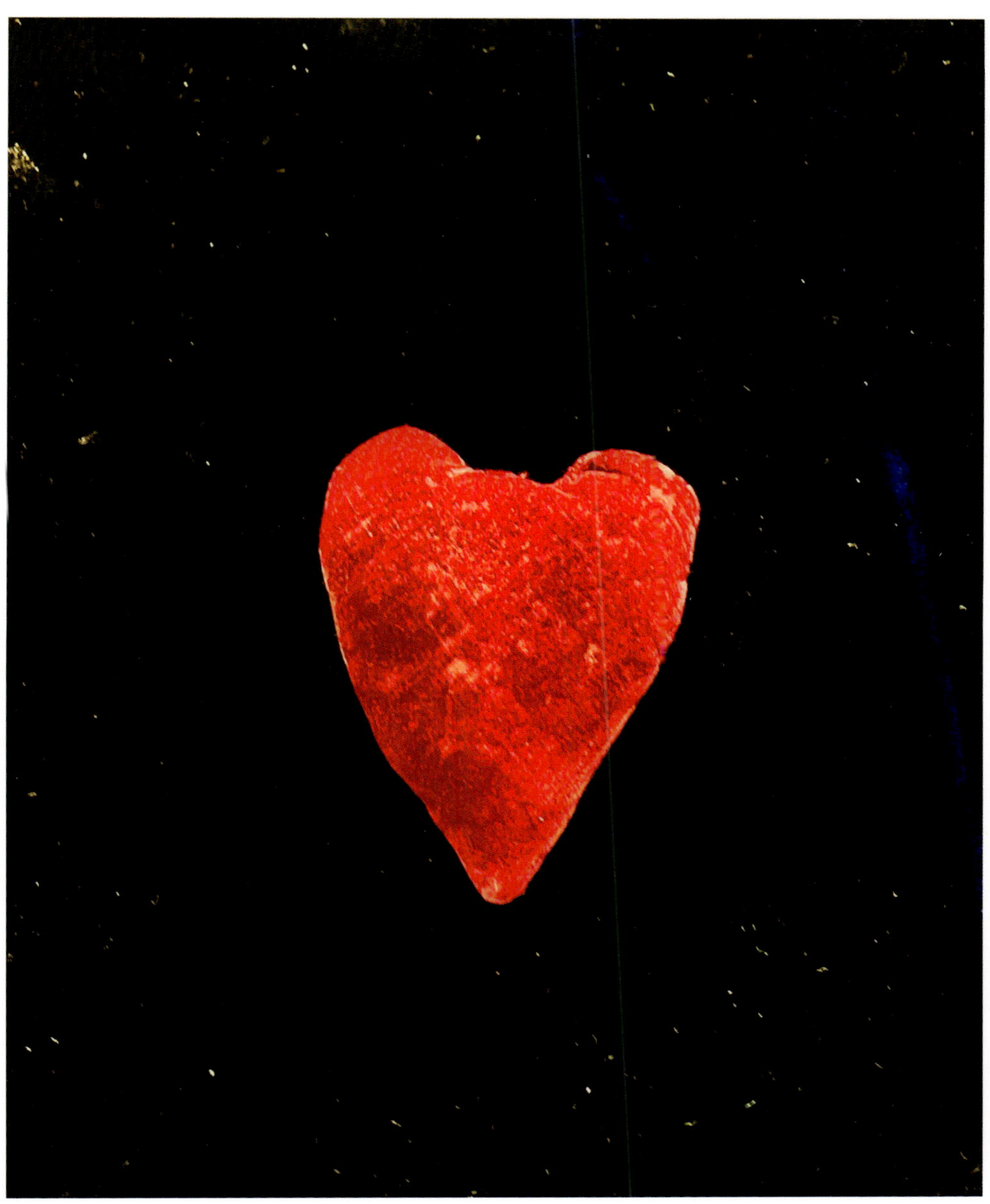

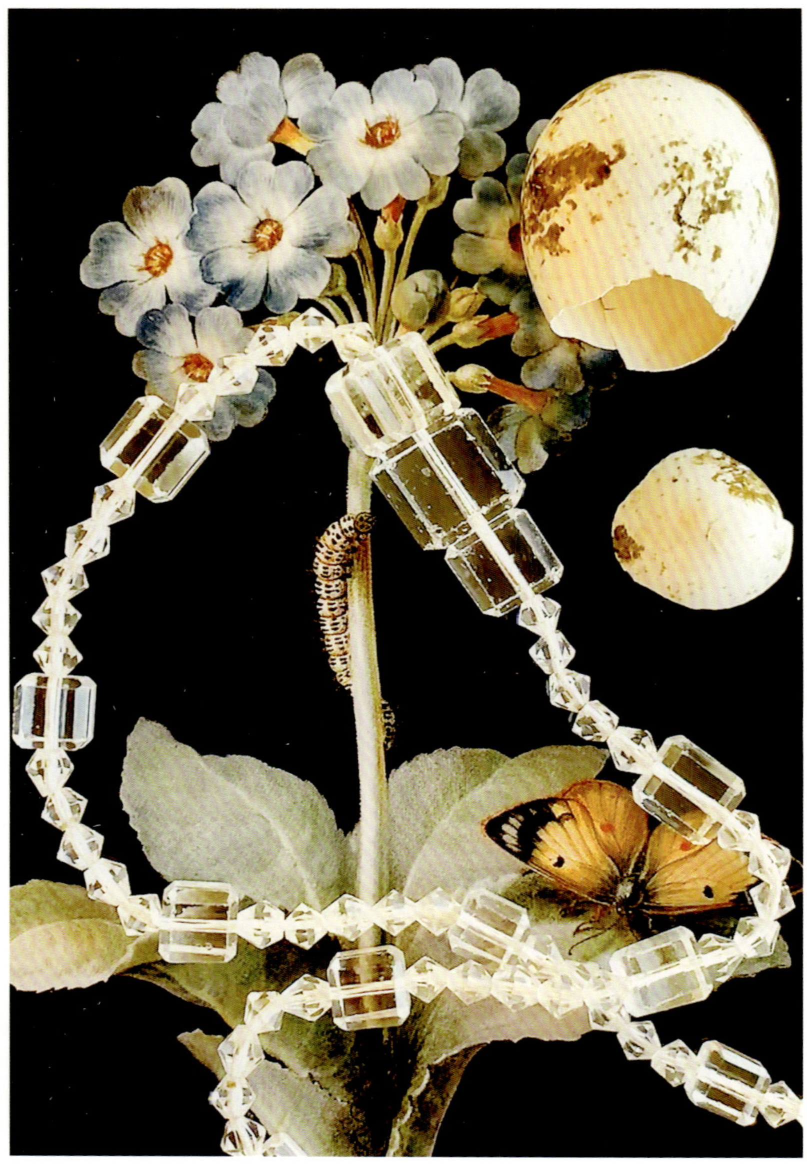

A chick was born and a caterpillar became a butterfly. What do you plan to do today?

—background by Barbara Dietzsch (1706–1783)

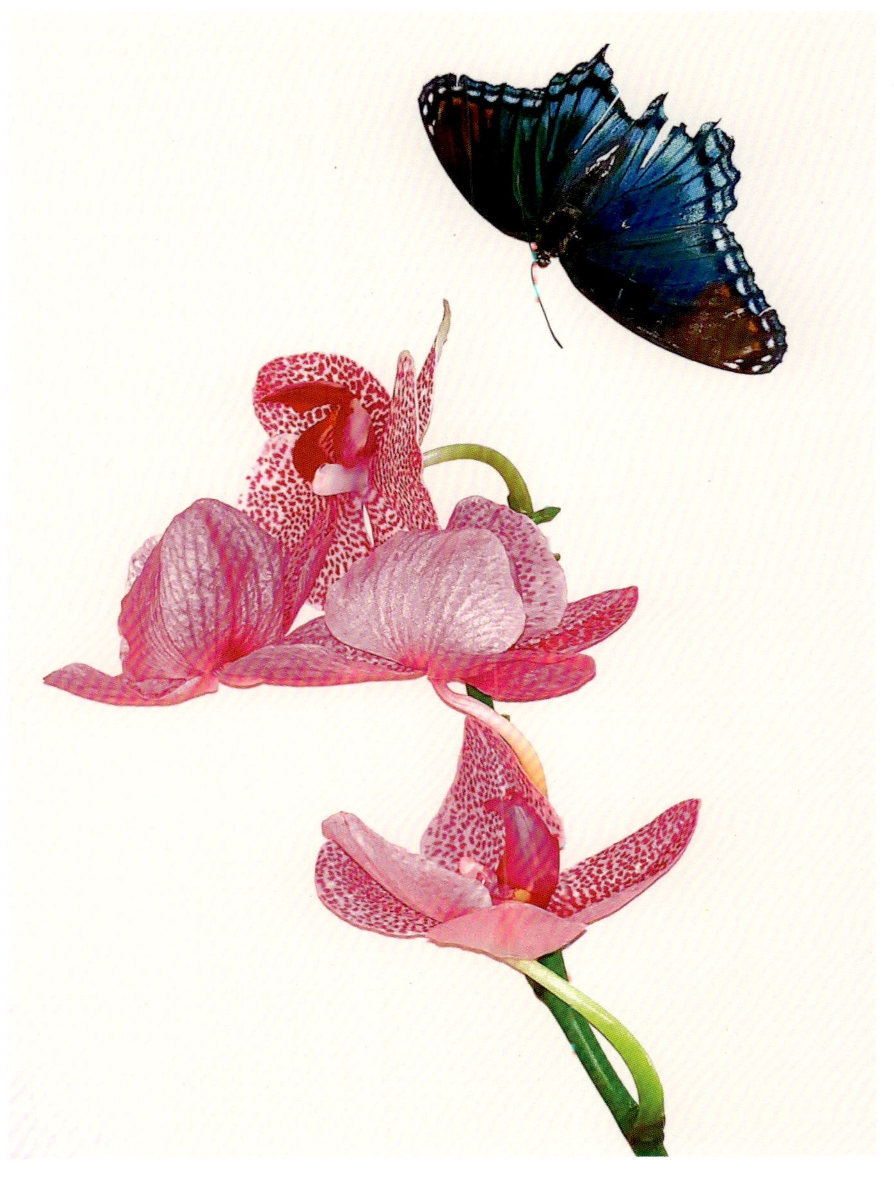

You must change your life!

—Rainer Maria Rilke

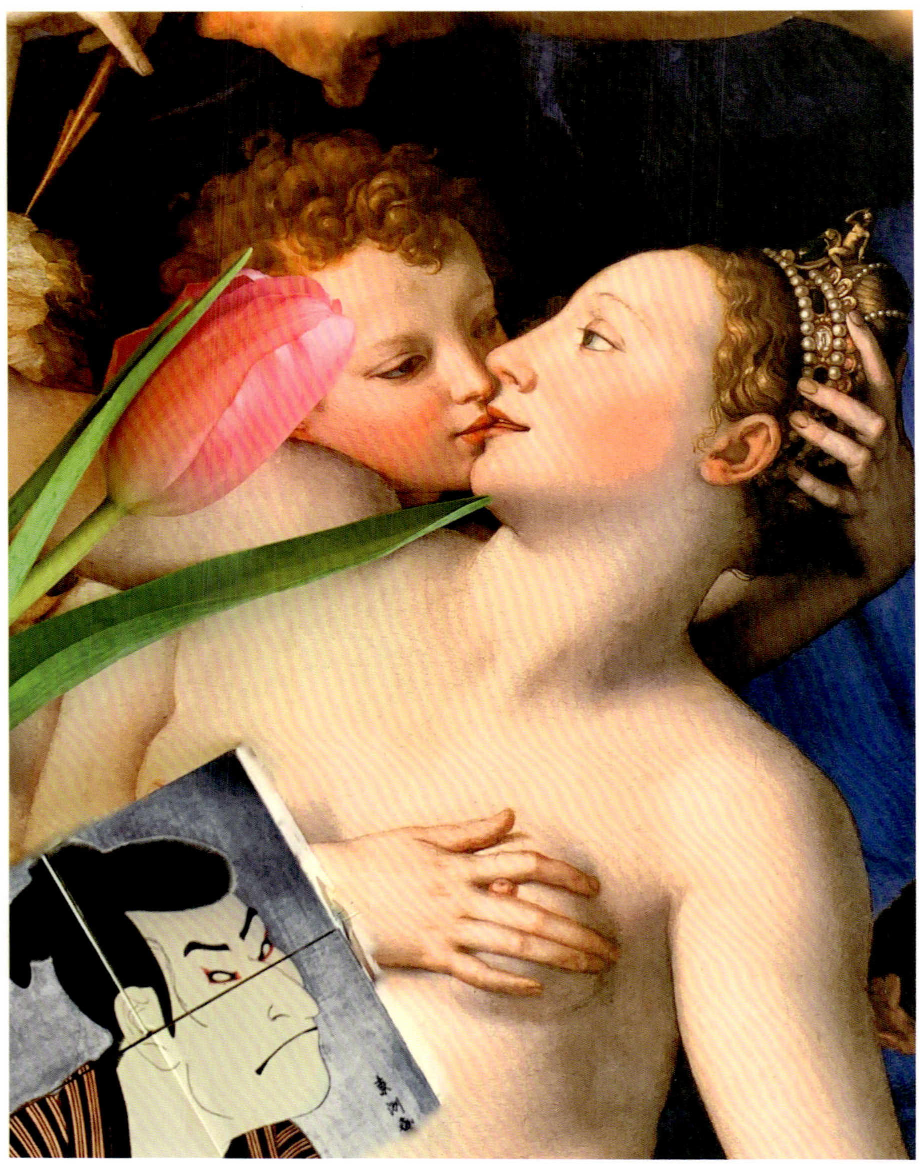

You silly boy who feels clever to be playing an instrument so fine as I am.
I will accommodate, and build your skill.

—Allegory of Venus and Cupid, *Agnolo di Cosimo (Bronzino), c.1545*

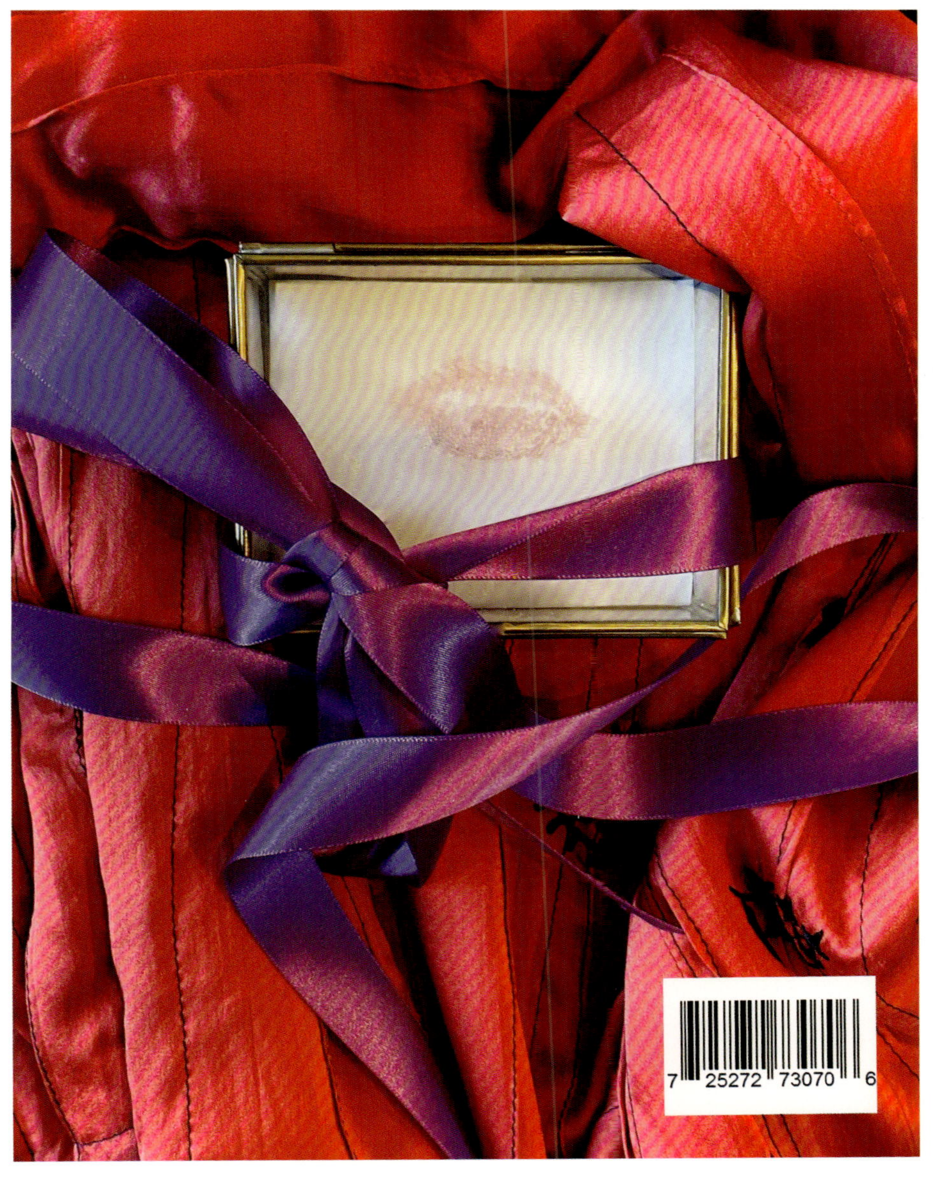

Kisses delayed burst like fermented fruit, or dry to dust.

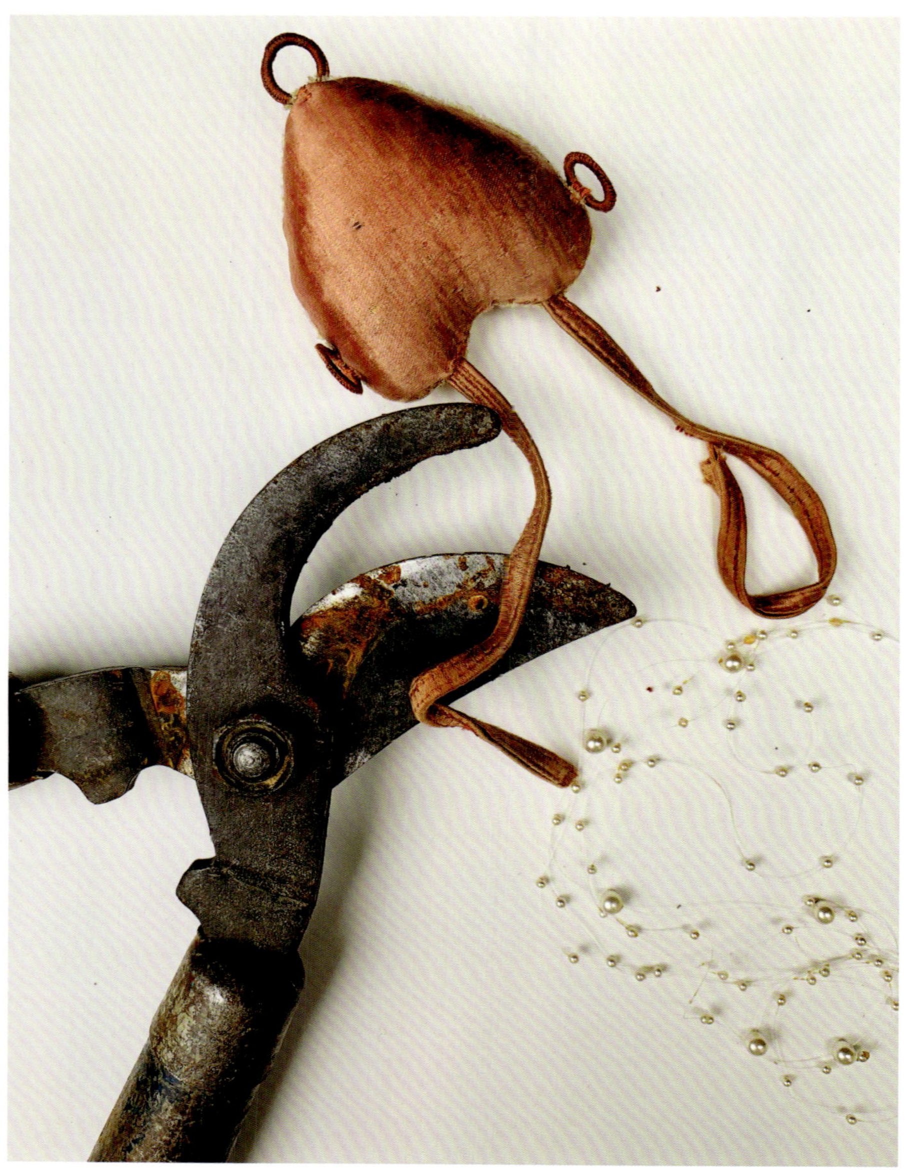

I softened myself for you, silkened myself for you. Now you cut out my heart.
I found your ferociousness intriguing. Now you will learn of mine.

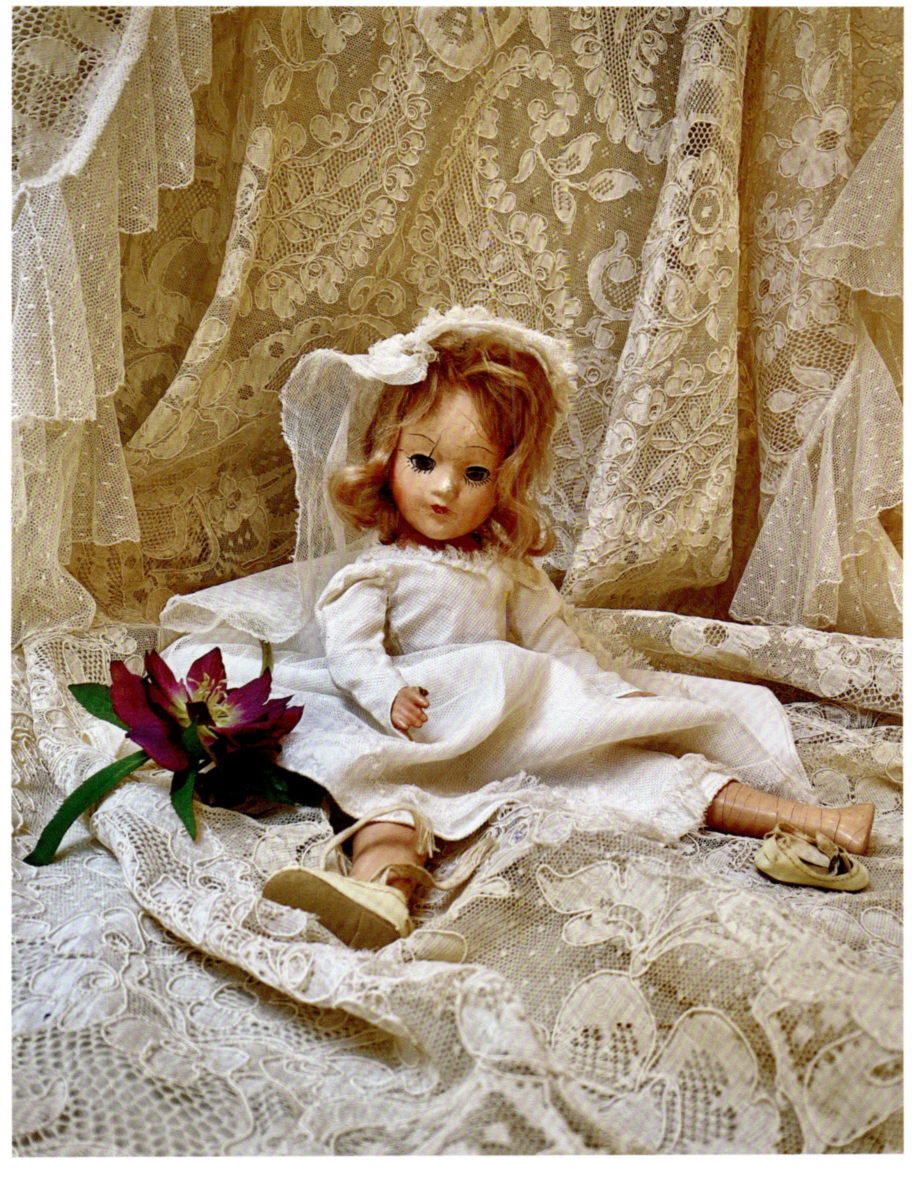

Her mother went from household to household telling the neighbors the wedding was canceled.

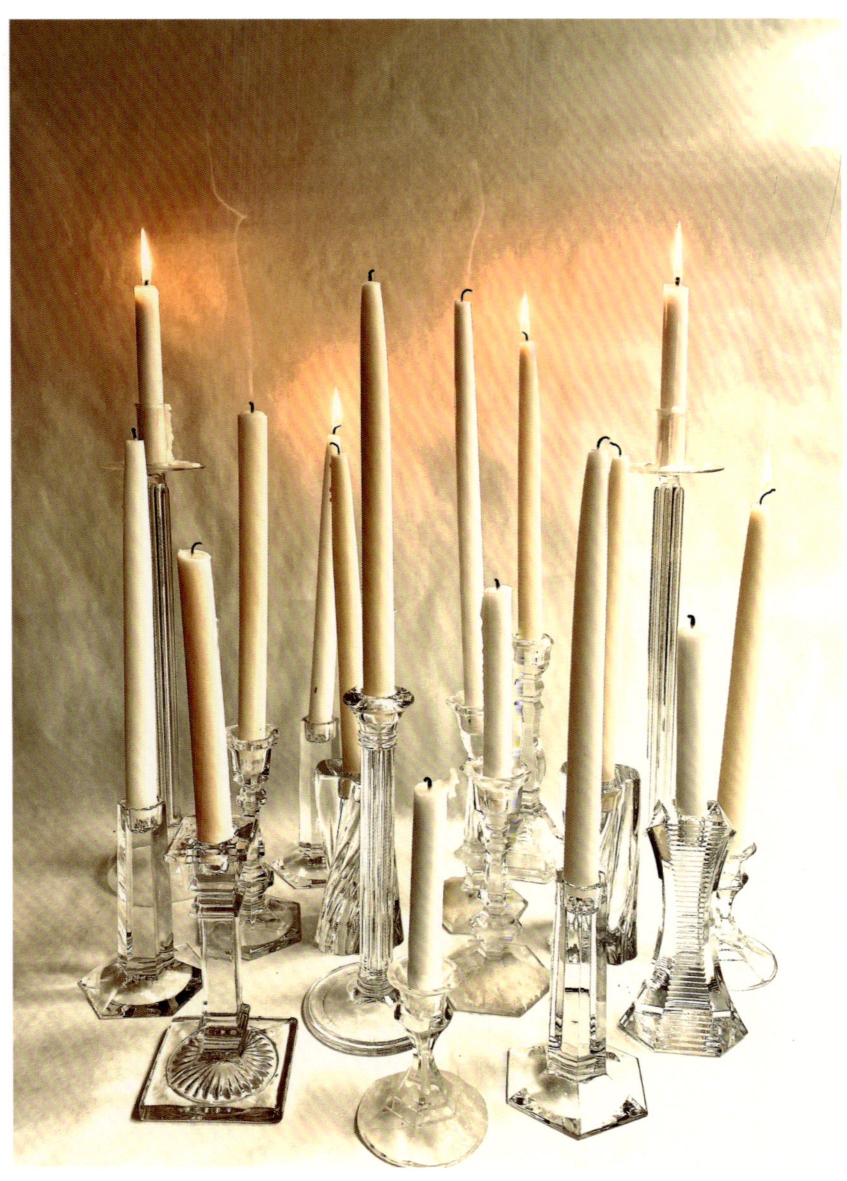

Candles have one story—light!

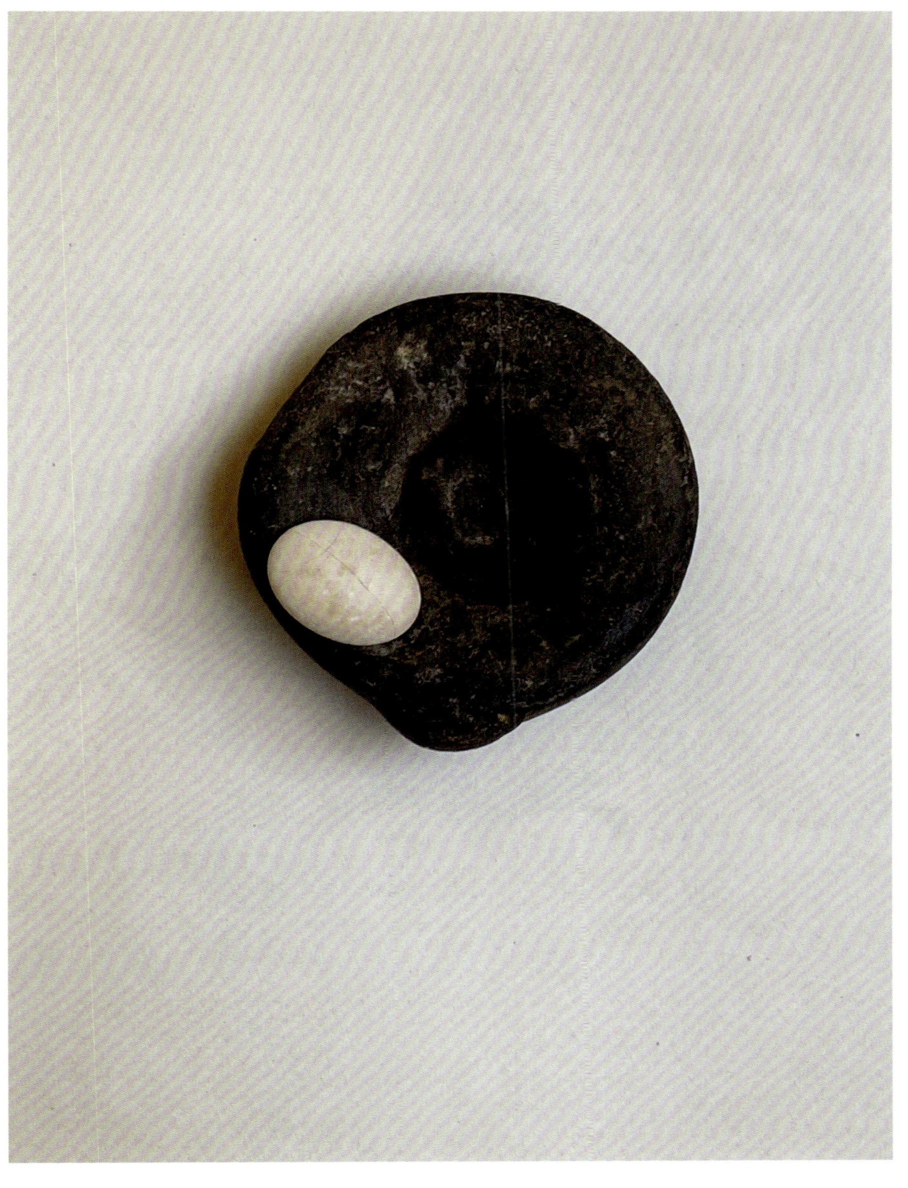

Native American fire starter found by a spring fed creek.

—hollowed out rock 1 ½" diameter from Tennessee; white pebble from beach in Italy

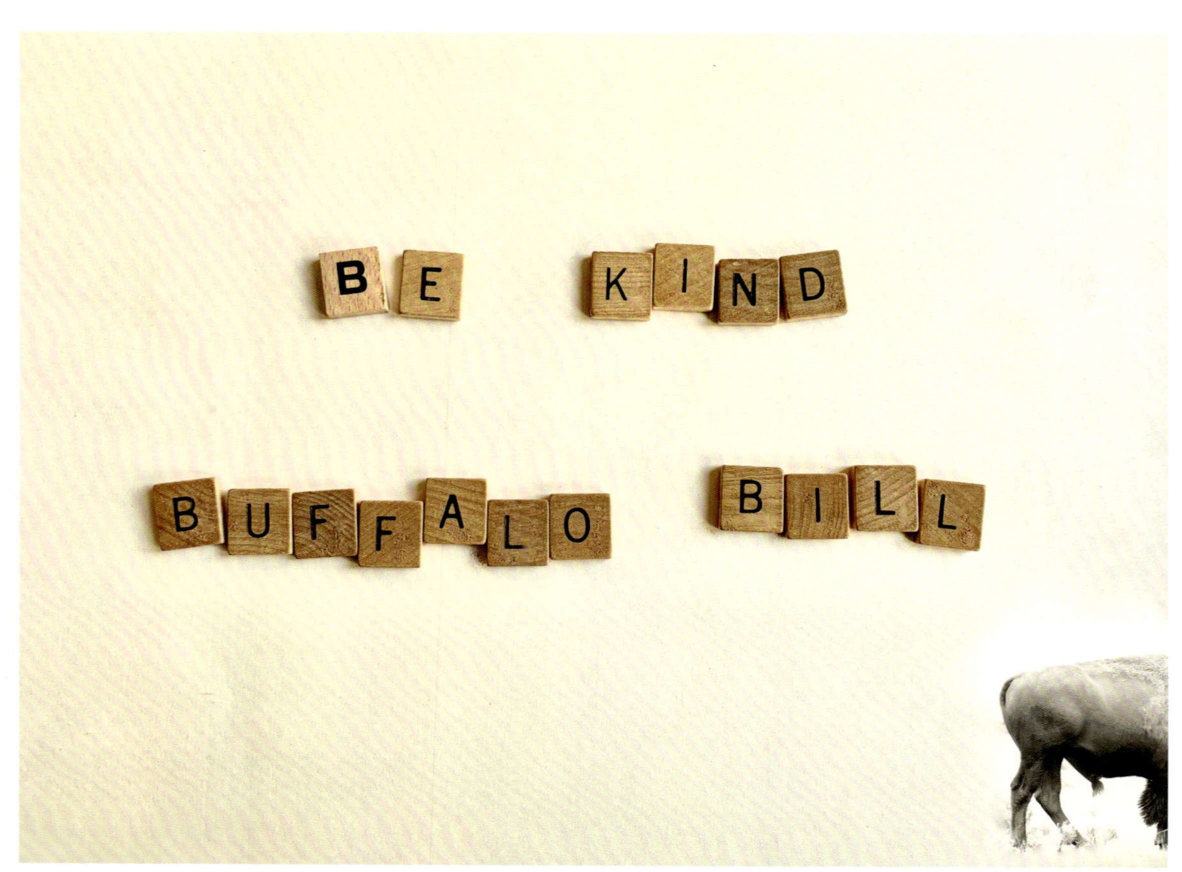

Destruction erodes souls through generations.

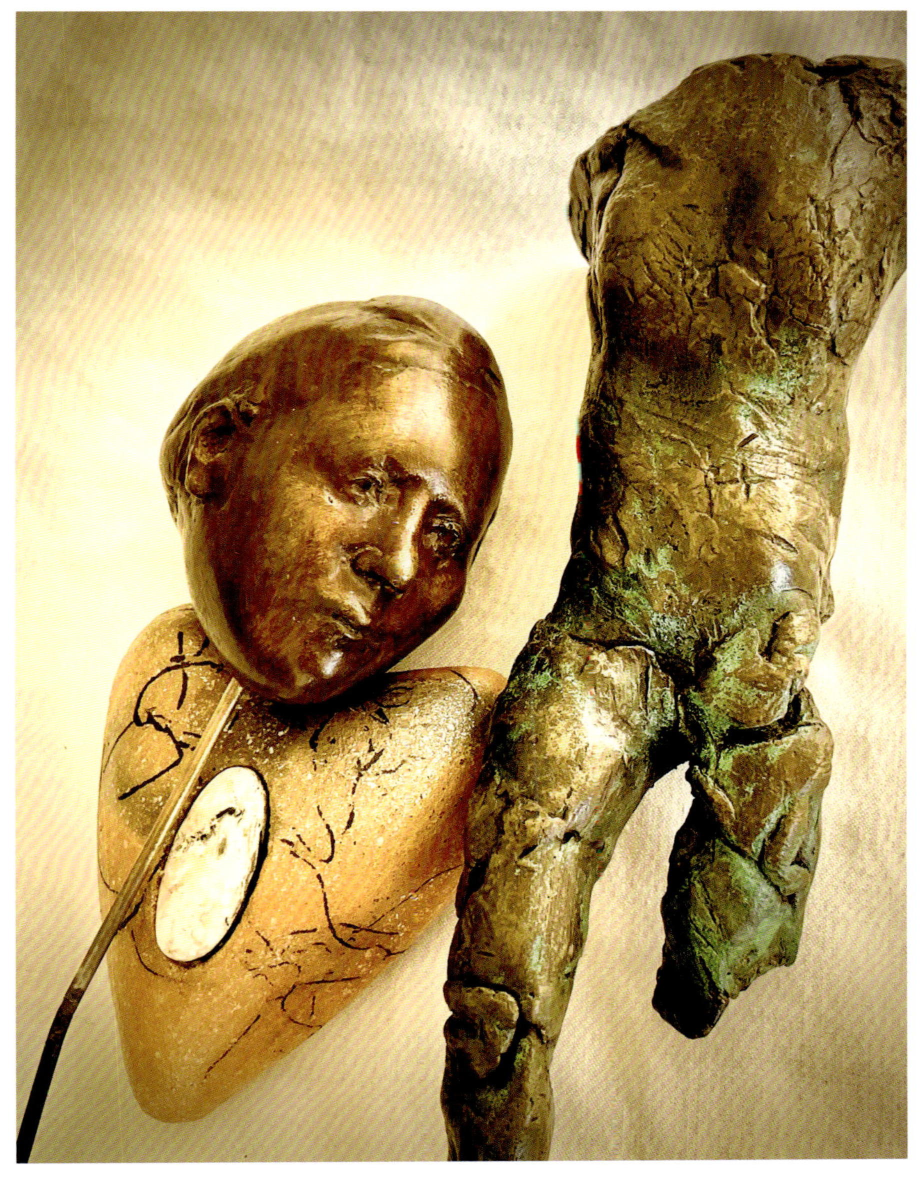

Our blood stained the snow red at Wounded Knee, but do not be proud.
The ground remembers us, we will never die.

— Head by Charles Matton, c. 1970; heart by Richard Oliver, 2018; torso by William Dunlap, 1995

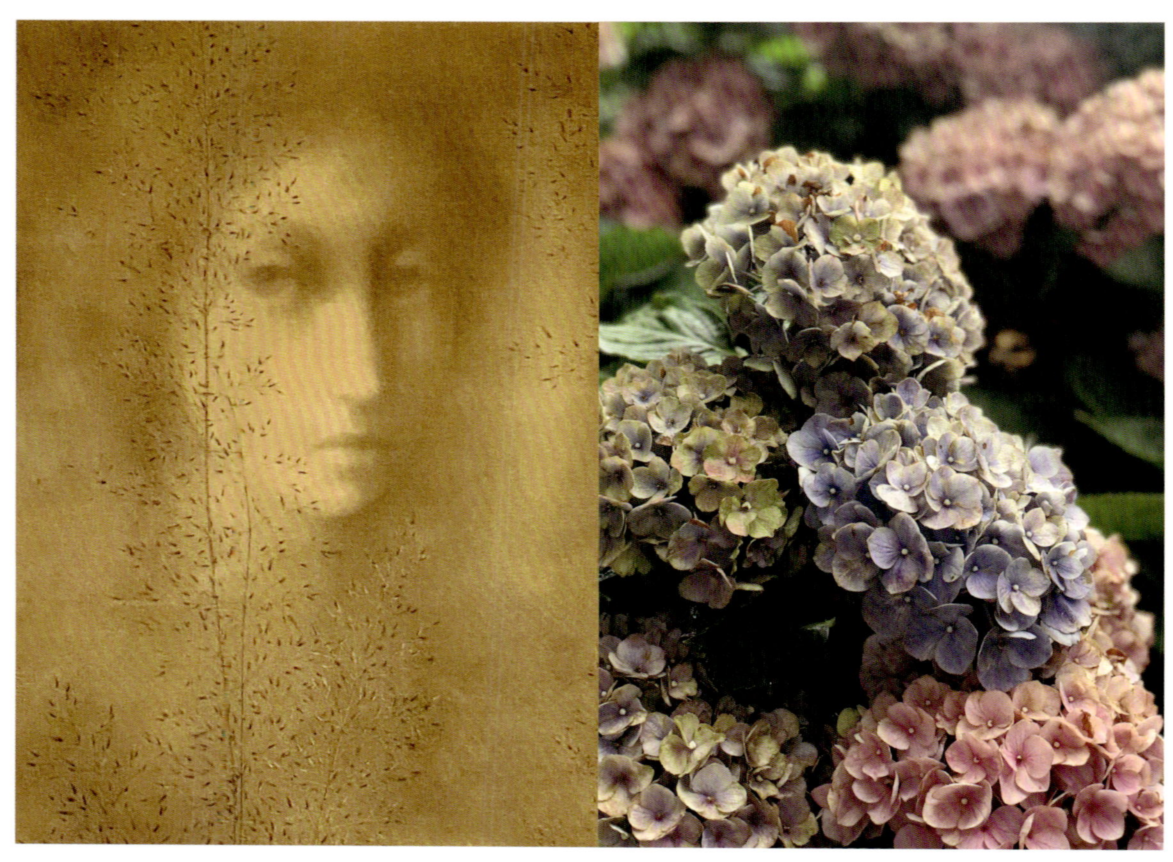

The woman and the hydrangeas gave me faith to wake each morning during the year of grief.

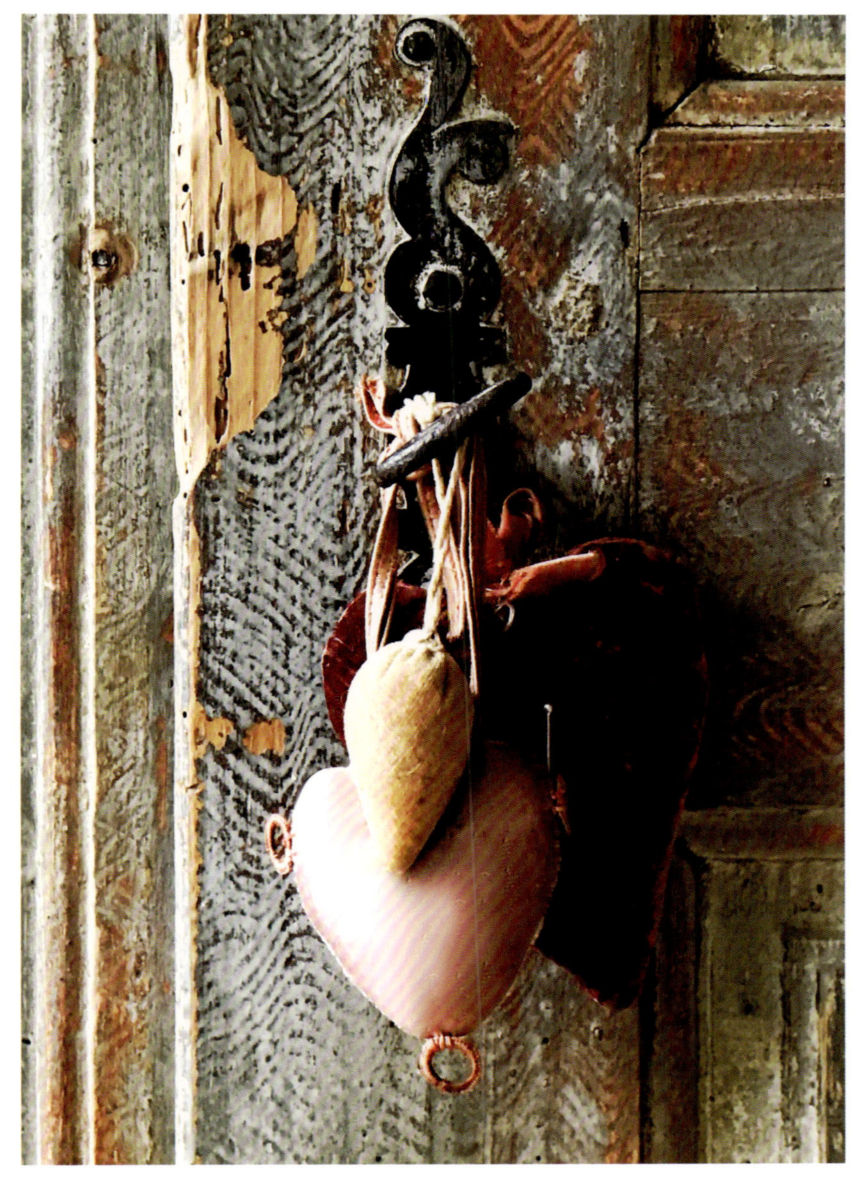

If you do not understand this photo...

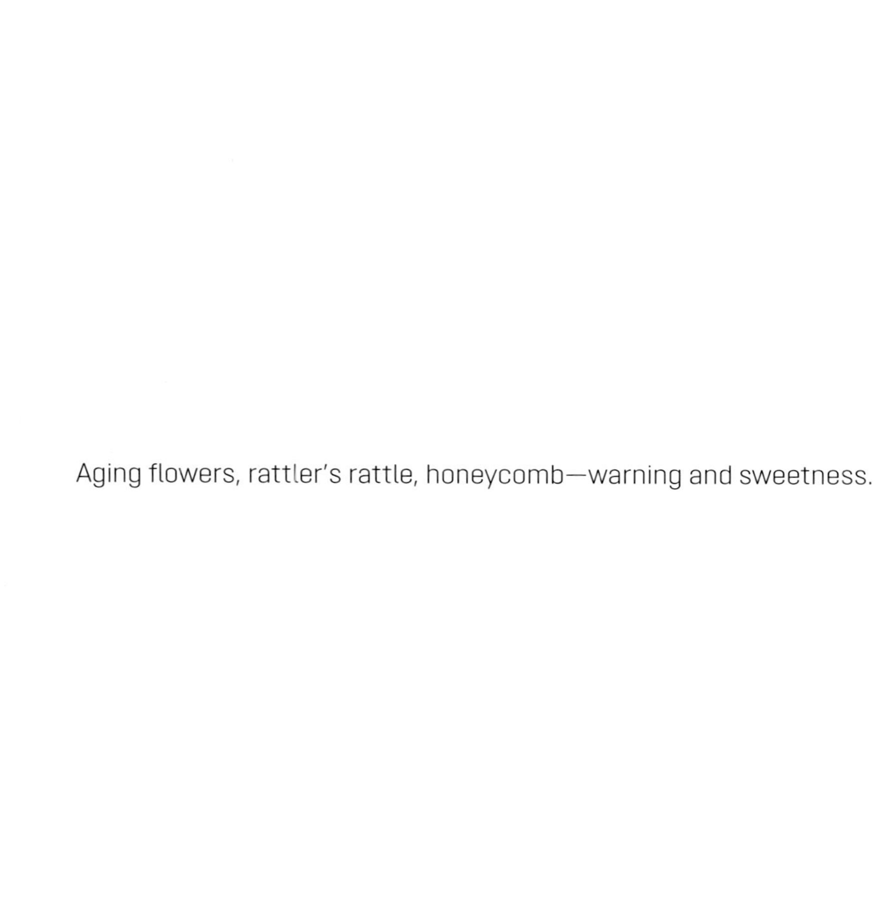

Aging flowers, rattler's rattle, honeycomb—warning and sweetness.

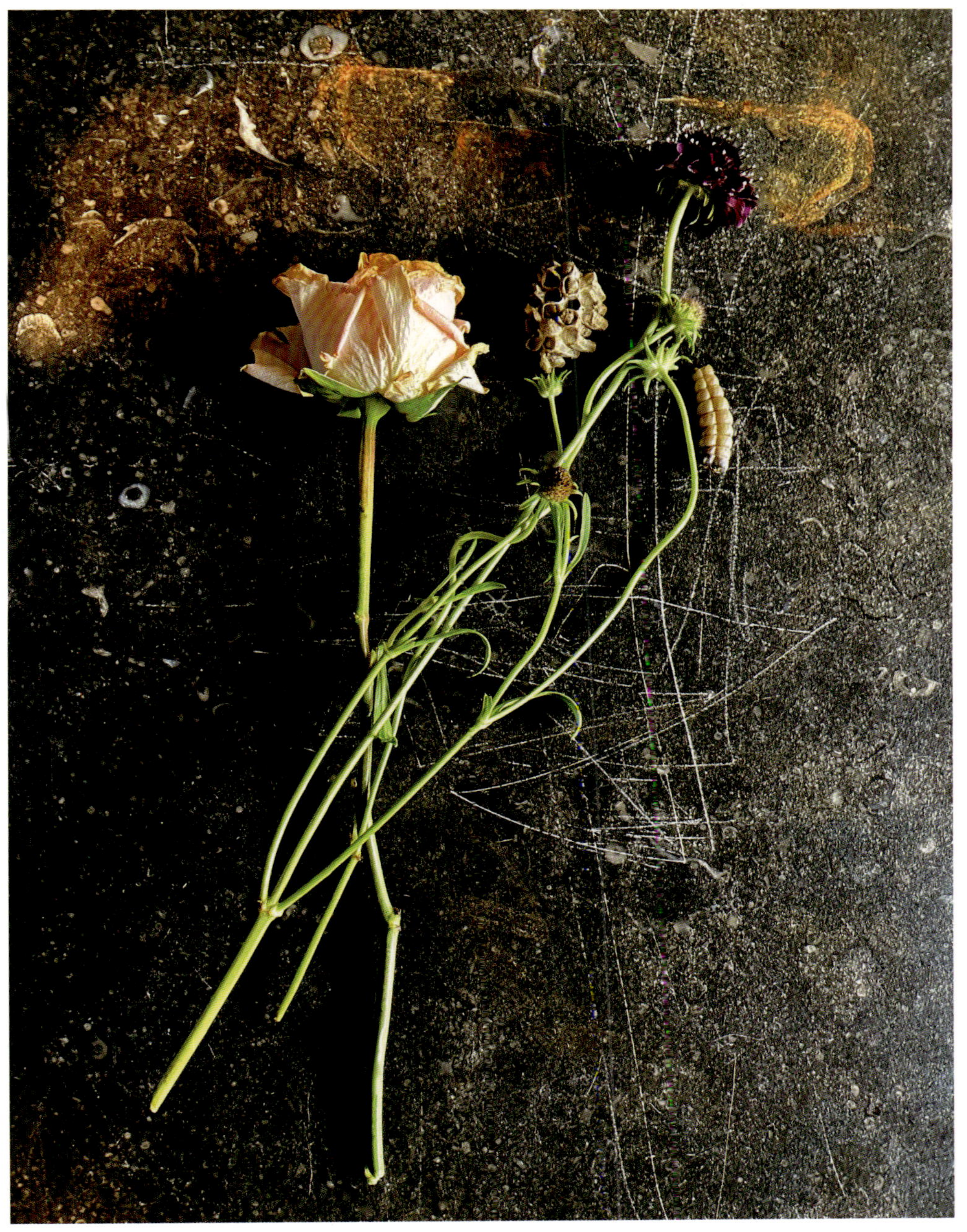

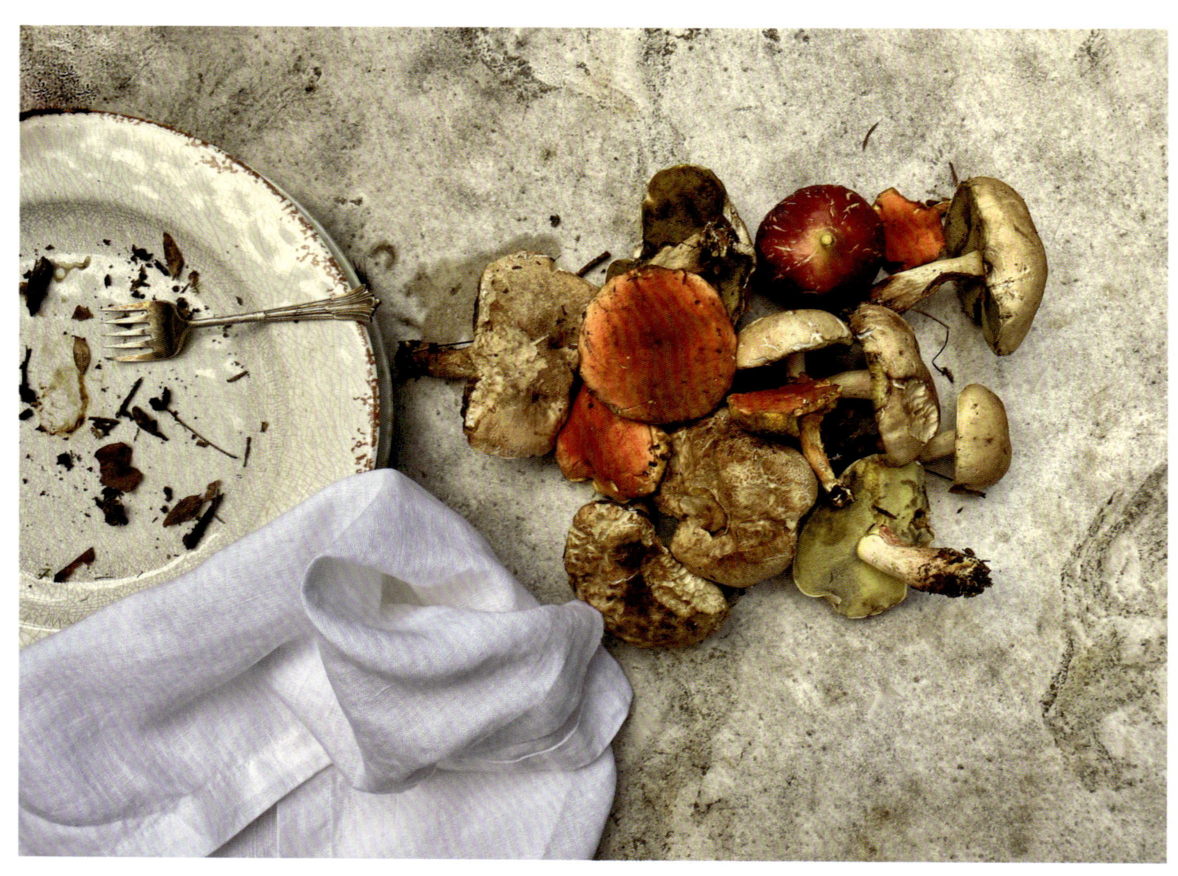

What feeds, what deceives, and what expands reality can be from the same family
—mushrooms, for example.

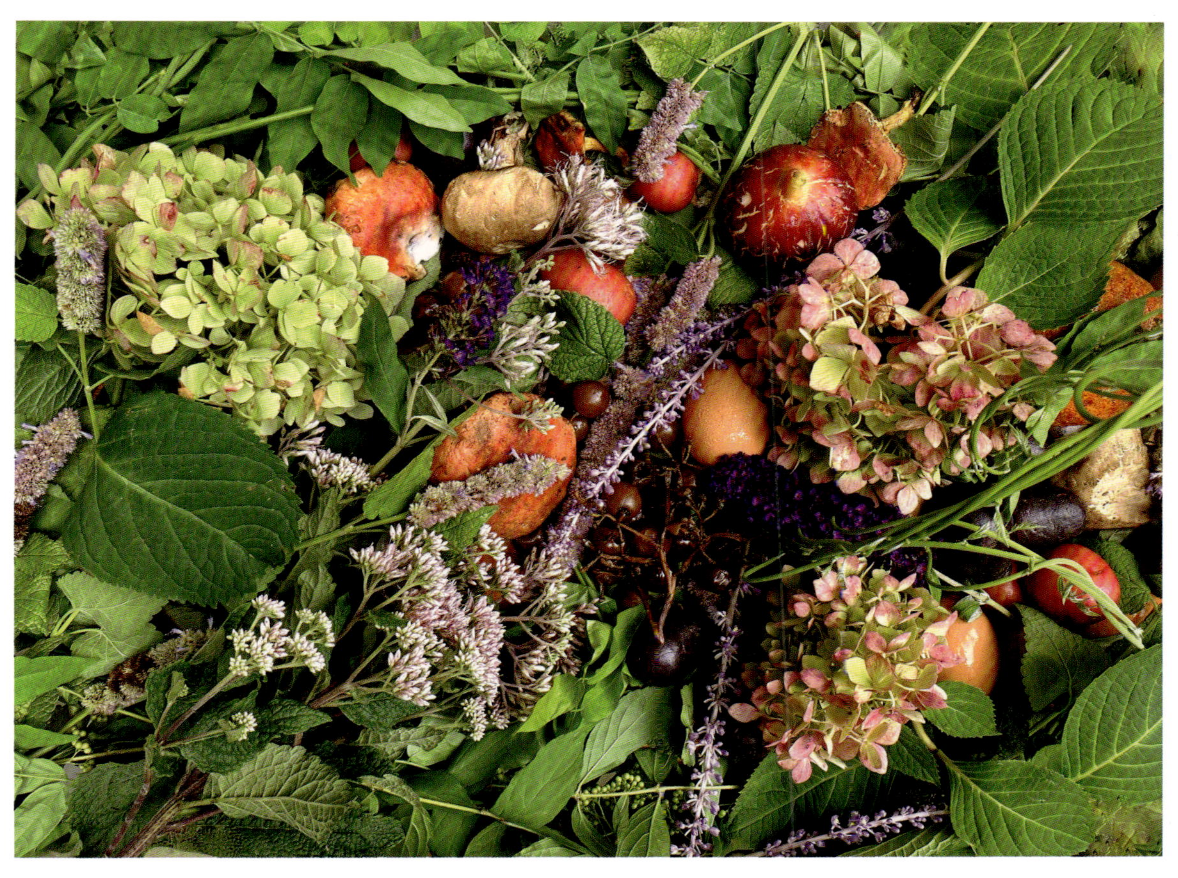

Autumn brings nature's more somber gifts, those with gravitas and unique personalities.
They carry the bounty of a full season.

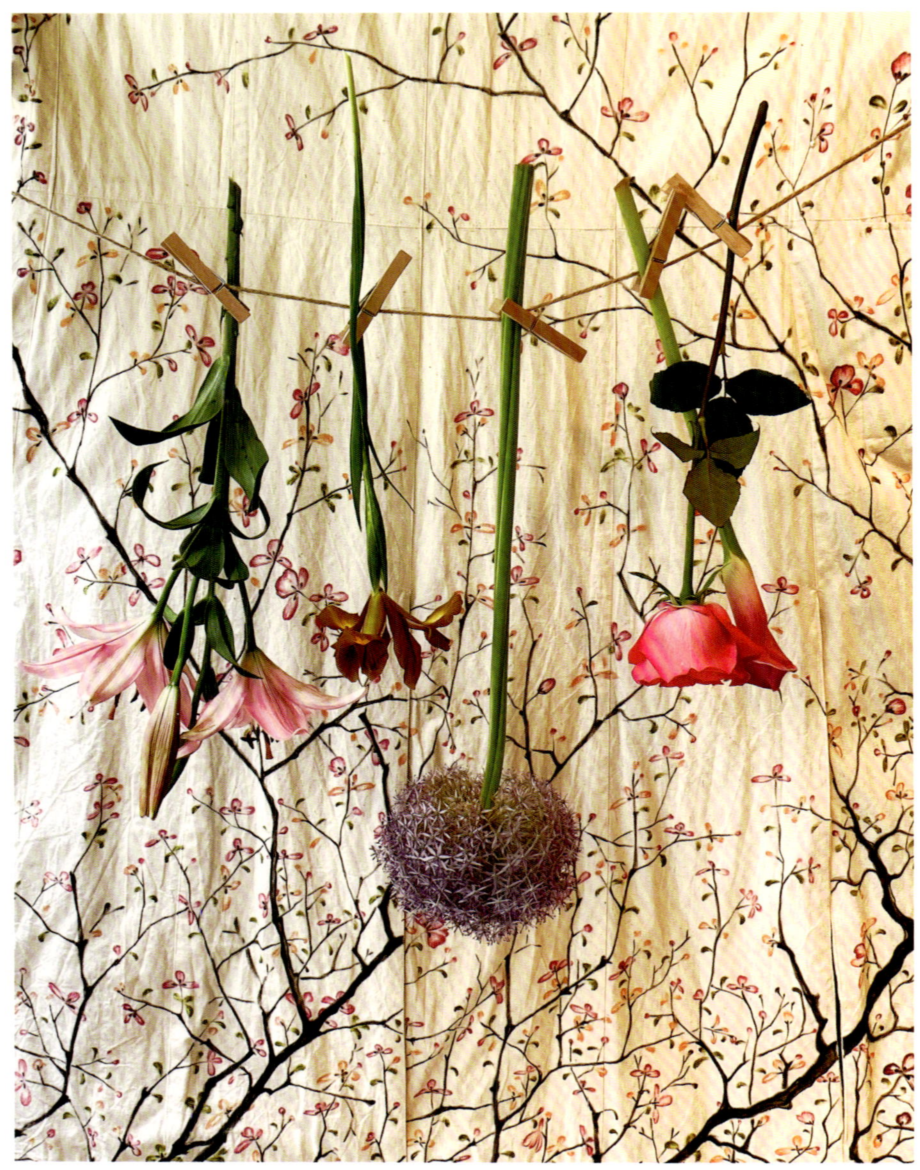

Bathe in the rain, kiss petals, rejoice when nothing makes sense.

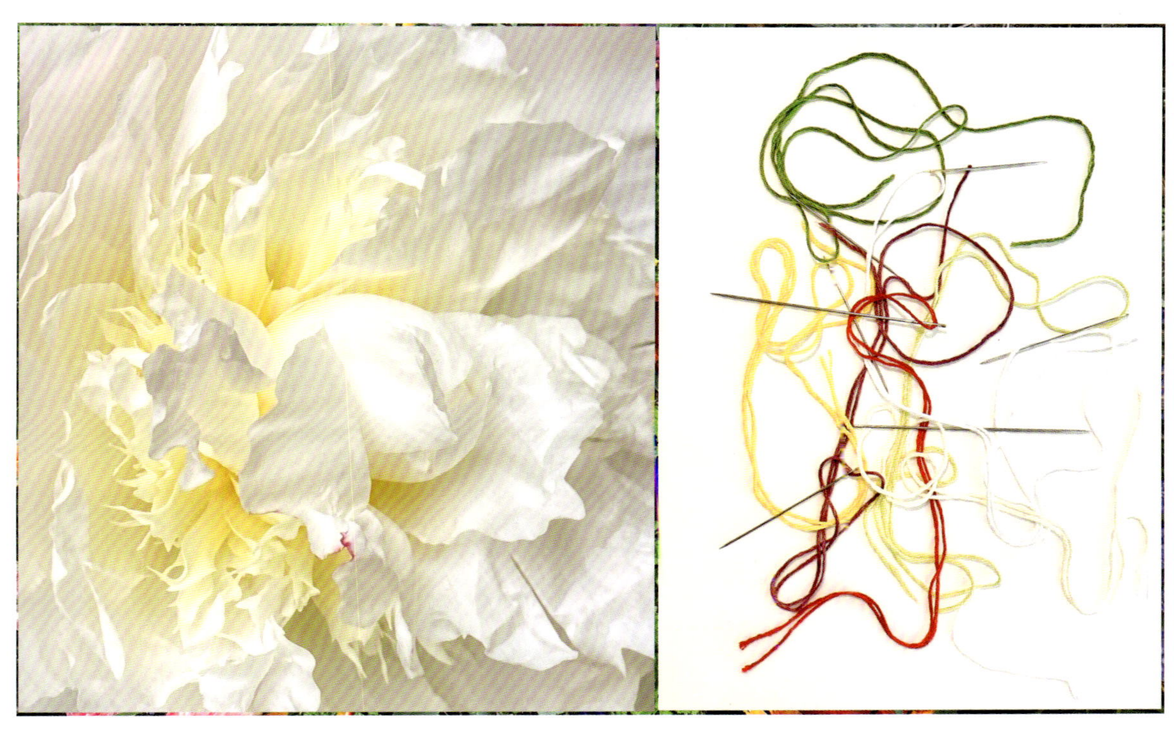

Tend what needs tending, prune what is greedy.
Let beauty pierce you sharp as a needle.

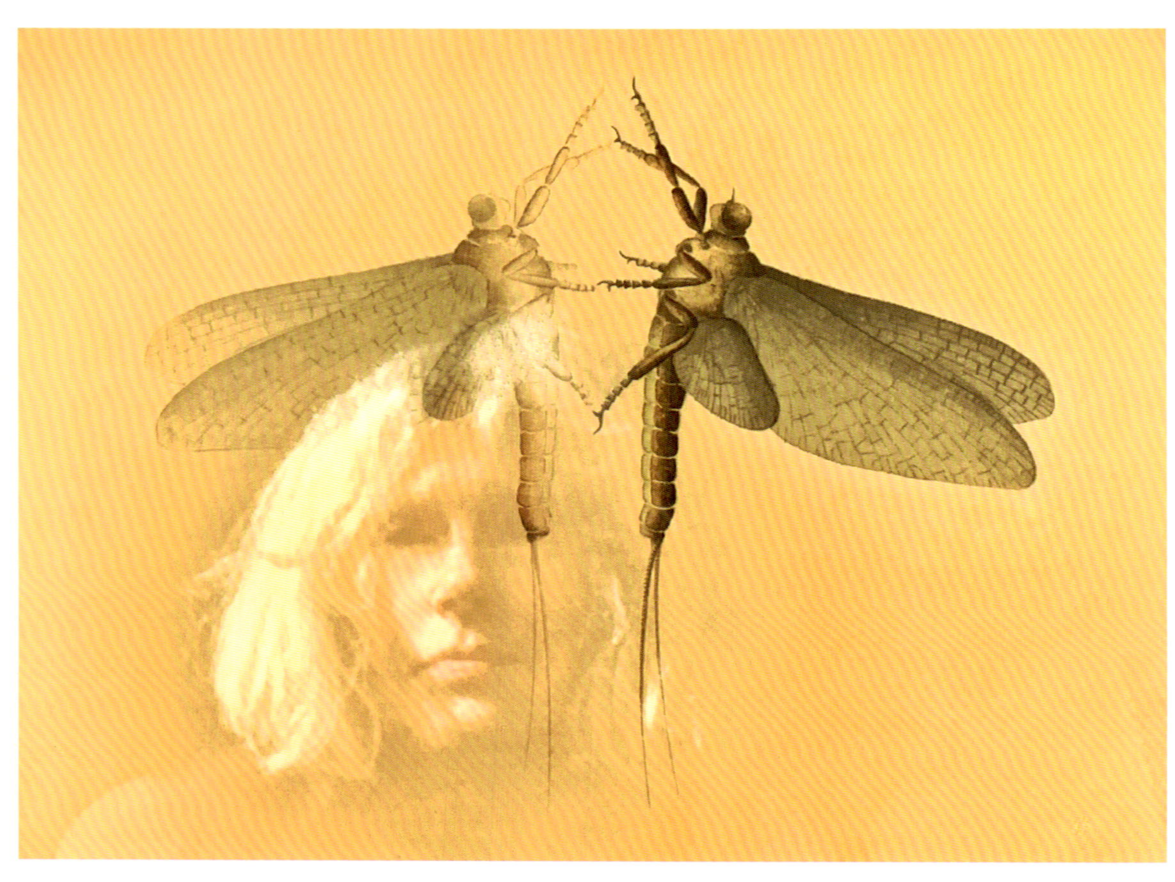

I am. I am here on this earth with you in this mystery of not knowing.
This is my gift to you—my gesture.

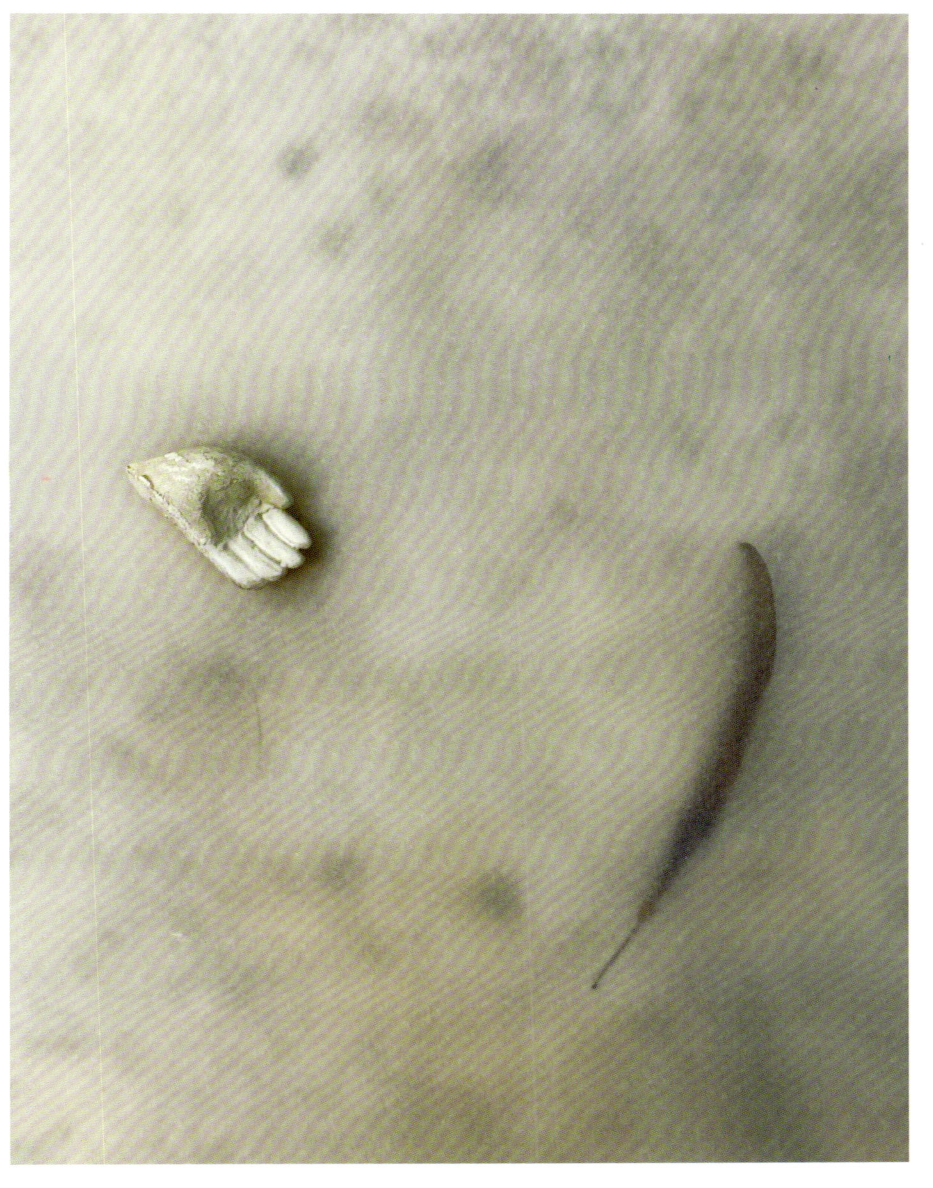

Pray with your hands open.

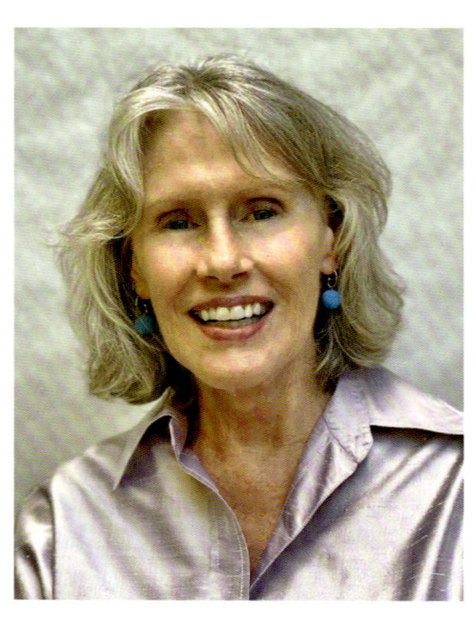

Patricia Z. Smith

Three forces have driven Patricia Smith's careers and life—the search for the underpinnings of our existence, the imperative to see and create beauty, and the obligation to work for a better world.

Arriving to Washington, DC from Iowa at 21 with no job and borrowed money, she became the photographer for the Office of Economic Opportunity and created a photo archive of poverty and programs across the US. She taught photography with the Smithsonian Adult Education Program and had numerous exhibitions of her work.

She was an award-winning playwright and vintage quilt dealer with her collection of rare pre-1850 quilts exhibited by the Smithsonian American Arts Museum. In 2002 she founded and directed the first social network-based NGO. Peace X Peace connected women in the US for secure private conversations with women in more than 120 nations. She was editor, photographer, and interviewer for the book *Sixty Years, Sixty Voices: Israeli and Palestinian Women* and executive director of the award-winning documentary *Peace by Peace: Women on the Frontlines* filmed in Afghanistan, Bosnia, Burundi, Argentina, and the US. The film debuted at the UN and was aired on PBS.

Having been married and divorced three times, she is content to hang out with her family and friends, tend her garden, and keep company with small objects that speak to her and for her.

Gratitudes

Louise Brody, you brought your years of experience to designing our book. Still more, you brought your meticulous care, unerring eye, and high spirits. You made our collaboration between Paris and Washington, DC a joy in the time of a pandemic. The "small objects" thank you and I thank you—deeply.

Gordon Goff, you recognized the essence of *COMPLEMENTS* immediately. Then you, Jake Anderson, and the rest of the expert team at Goff Books turned it into a reality needed for these times. I remain amazed and grateful.

David Hume Kennerly, you call yourself an old-fashioned news photographer, yet you saw my "small objects" and heard their tales. The foreword you wrote captured those spritely characters, for which I am thankful. They can be a handful.

Most of the "small objects" were ones that came my way over decades, but a scrappy team of "outside suppliers" brought new treasures—Angela Calos a shark tooth fossil and tarty pie server, Oobie Gleysteen and Patricia Lloyd silk Chinese slippers, Jill McGovern pastel hen eggs, and Richard Oliver glass eyes, paring knife, sphinx moth, and rattlesnake rattle. Their joy in sleuthing mattered more than they knew.

My Facebook friends are writers, poets, photographers, and painters from around the world. They inspire me daily with their work, their responses to mine, and their encouragement. You know who you are. Thank you.

My family and friends have created a nest around me that enables me to live in a world of love and creativity. I need and cherish you.

Goff Books
Published by Goff Books. An Imprint of ORO Editions
Gordon Goff: Publisher

www.goffbooks.com
info@goffbooks.com

Text and Photography: Patricia Z. Smith / www.patriciazsmith.com
Design: Louise Brody / www.louisebrodydesign.com
Managing Editor: Jake Anderson

10 9 8 7 6 5 4 3 2 1 First Edition

ISBN: 978-1-951541-74-3

Color Separations and Printing: ORO Group Ltd.
Printed in China.

Goff Books makes a continuous effort to minimize the overall carbon footprint of its publications. As part of this goal, Goff Books, in association with Global ReLeaf, arranges to plant trees to replace those used in the manufacturing of the paper produced for its books. Global ReLeaf is an international campaign run by American Forests, one of the world's oldest nonprofit conservation organizations. Global ReLeaf is American Forests' education and action program that helps individuals, organizations, agencies, and corporations improve the local and global environment by planting and caring for trees.